FRENCH PHILADELPHIA

FRENCH PHILADELPHIA

The French Cultural & Historical Presence in the Delaware Valley

* * * * *

Lynn H. Miller & Annette H. Emgarth

Photography by Emmanuel Pierre Gee

* * * * *

*Published for the Alliance Française
de Philadelphie
by*

Beach Lloyd
PUBLISHERS
LLC

WAYNE, PENNSYLVANIA

Beach Lloyd Publishers, April 2006
Copyright © 2006 by the Alliance Française de Philadelphie
Second printing, 2007

Library of Congress Cataloging-in-Publication Data

Miller, Lynn H.
 French Philadelphia : the French cultural & historical presence in the Delaware Valley / Lynn H. Miller & Annette H. Emgarth; photography by Emmanuel Pierre Gee.
  p. cm.
 Summary: "An illustrated guide for visitors and residents alike, documenting the French cultural and historical presence in Philadelphia and the Delaware Valley, both yesterday and today. Tangible evidence of the historical and philosophical ties between France and the United States—ties dating from the birth of the new nation to the present"—Provided by publisher.
 Includes bibliographical references and index.
 ISBN 978-0-9743158-8-1 (pbk. : alk. paper)
 1. French Americans—Pennsylvania—Philadelphia Region—History.
 2. Philadelphia Region (Pa.)—Civilization. 3. United States—Civilization—French influences. 4. Philadelphia Region (Pa.)—Biography. 5. Philadelphia Region (Pa.)—Guidebooks. 6. Historic buildings—Pennsylvania—Philadelphia Region—Guidebooks.
 7. Philadelphia (Pa.)—Guidebooks. I. Emgarth, Annette H., 1900-1992. II. Alliance française de Philadelphie. III. Title.
 F158.9.F8M55 2006
 974.8'11004'1–dc22
                                                    2006005317

Cover design by Kevin Bugge;
Book design by Joanne S. Silver;
Technical direction by Ronald Silver.

Cover photo: The Rodin Museum entrance and *Le Penseur [The Thinker]* by sculptor Auguste Rodin (1840-1917). Located on the Benjamin Franklin Parkway in Philadelphia, Pennsylvania.

In memory of Jeannette P. Kean,
who loved the French language, literature, music and culture.

French Philadelphia

CONTENTS

PREFACE

Jean-David Levitte
Ambassador of France to the United States of America

Since its foundation in 1682, Philadelphia, the "City of Brotherly Love," has always appealed to the French people.

In its very early days, many thousands of French of all origins made their way to the city, attracted by the religious and political freedoms they were offered here. During the 18th century, the development in France and in Europe of the philosophical movement drew increased attention to the social experiments taking place in Philadelphia, often seen as the cradle of liberty, with a cosmopolitan community thriving on tolerance and individual freedom. The fame of Philadelphia grew even further when it sent to Paris Benjamin Franklin, the first Ambassador of America to France, who played a critical role in securing the French support and alliance to the insurgents in their quest for liberty and independence, but who was also highly regarded in the Parisian society of the Age of Enlightenment as a prominent scientist, a statesman and a distinguished philosopher.

With the French Revolution, in the aftermath of the end of Napoléon's Empire, Philadelphia continued to receive many French people, and their cultural, social, political heritage left deep impressions on Penn's town.

It is indeed, in my view, a most desirable experience to stroll around in the streets of Philadelphia, a city with a distinctive European flavor and way of life, and this guide book will help the visitor to trace, street by street, house by house, through a narrative tour of the town and its neighborhoods, the highlights of the French influence in Philadelphia.

The longstanding relations between Philadelphia and France continue to extend today. The modern city, a post-industrial center with advanced health services, higher education and high tech industries, has attracted the most important concentration of direct French investment in the USA, with such companies as Sanofi Aventis, St. Gobain, Sartomer and Arkema. And the French presence is also supported by a well-integrated French community of 5000, several very active Franco-American societies and, of course, many French restaurants around Rittenhouse Row, the lively French quarter.

From 1682 down to 2006, four centuries of reciprocal fascination laid the solid foundations of the relations between Philadelphia and France. And there's more to come . . .

PREFACE

Danièle L. Thomas Easton, Honorary Consul of France
in Philadelphia and Wilmington, 1996-2005,
current Director France - Philadelphie

At the risk of paraphrasing Josephine Baker, the American soul of jazz music who, in the 30's, was singing in France « J'ai deux amours, mon pays et Paris », I am tempted to add "I have two loves, my country and Philly," a sentiment that French expatriates in Philadelphia all share! For Philadelphia holds a very special place in my heart. And it is through my association with the Alliance Française that I have made so many discoveries about my adopted city.

As a newcomer, I was stunned to see, on the very Rittenhouse Square where I live, a sculpture by the 19th century French artist Antoine-Louis Barye, the same sculptor whose *Lion* greets visitors when they enter Musée d'Orsay and whose *Lion au Serpent* graces the Louvre and the Tuileries Garden. What to say of my surprise when first spotting the statue of Joan of Arc near the Art Museum, the original cast of only three existing editions by Emmanuel Fremiet who, through an adroit maneuver of legerdemain which he never disclosed to the French authorities, gave us the original cast?

Then I found at the Alliance Française this jewel of a book by Annette Emgarth, *French Philadelphia*, a delightful, whimsical collection of anecdotes mixing history and stories, revealing an extensive range of intriguing and little known details of architectural, diplomatic, historical and economic connections between France and our city. With this "French primer," visiting the city was no longer a traditional routine, but a way to see Philadelphia afresh through the prism of French immigration, through the kaleidoscope of atypical and elaborate information all related to the French presence here. It was meeting all over the city with French phantoms of the past, still hovering around us and retelling us, in hushed words, the long links of French-American amity.

Miss Annette Emgarth, whom I have been privileged to know, was passionate and committed to uncovering fascinating French facts not even familiar to most Philadelphians. Her book was a true labor of love. « L'amour, toujours l'amour » ! she would repeat, punctuating her lectures with her principal explanation for any prolonged sojourn made in Philadelphia by a French visitor. To balance the exuberance of Miss Emgarth, the Alliance Française needed someone with a strong dose of Cartesian discipline, a rigor in research, to bring forth a new edition of this treasure, and drew upon the research talents of Board member and retired professor Lynn Miller. We are now all very indebted to him for lending his professional skills to the task of combing diligently through documents and research in order to give us a new version of *French Philadelphia*.

Linking the past to the present, Lynn Miller's *French Philadelphia* continues to glorify the city's French connections, endearing it to French residents, to international visitors and, of course, to our American friends. It is most timely that the book goes to press this year, in 2006, at a time the City is celebrating the 300th anniversary of Benjamin Franklin, the first American Ambassador to France, to invite us to remember how the destinies of both countries have been woven together so intimately.

ACKNOWLEDGMENTS

*The Alliance Française de Philadelphie
is deeply grateful to Dr. Herbert Kean and his family
for making this publication possible.*

Many have contributed to the production of this new book. First among these is Nelly M. Childress, who has offered valued comments and suggestions while working diligently to translate the text for the forthcoming French edition of *French Philadelphia*. Hoi Ming Leung Guet's early enthusiasm for the project did much to persuade me to take it on. Members of the Board of Directors of the Alliance Française de Philadelphie have consistently shown their support. In particular, President Diana M. Regan, Danièle L. Thomas Easton, and Michael E. Scullin have all assisted me by giving of their time and energy. Martine Chauvet, Executive Director of the Alliance Française, has been unfailingly supportive and helpful, as has the rest of her staff. Joan Tedesco was an efficient and intelligent proof-reader of the manuscript. The Alliance Française is very grateful for the generosity of our printer, John Greene of KDPress.com. Joanne S. Silver has always been perceptive and insightful in her capacity as the book's editor.

Emmanuel Gee's photographs of the sites included were his generous contribution to this project and to the work of the Alliance Française. Thanks to Dr. Roger W. Moss, Executive Director of the Athenæum of Philadelphia, for his generosity in allowing us to reprint several eighteenth-century illustrations from the Athenæum's collection. I am also grateful to Ellen L. Rose and Bruce Laverty of the Athenæum's staff for their assistance in tracking down these and other materials. Charlene Peacock, of the Library Company of Philadelphia's Print Department, authorized reproduction of the broadside advertising du Simitiere's museum.

It is a pleasure to acknowledge here those companies that have assisted the Alliance Française de Philadelphie over the years. They include Air France, ARC International, Arkema, Inc., Just France, St. Gobain Corporation, Sartomer Company and USAirways. They have been true friends of the Alliance Française, and the Alliance remains grateful for their friendship.

French Philadelphia is largely about the warm ties that have long connected France to Philadelphia. In this three-hundredth anniversary of the birth of Philadelphia's most famous citizen, Benjamin Franklin, it is fitting to acknowledge him as the first Francophile among us. Without his efforts at the court of Louis XVI, it is doubtful that the insurrection waged by thirteen British colonies in North America would have ended in independence for the United States of America. Franklin succeeded in France largely because of the mutual respect and admiration that came about between him and the French people he met during the eight and a half years he was a resident in Paris. One of his frequent dinner companions there, the abbé Morellet, even composed a drinking song in Franklin's honor, setting it to a traditional French melody. With tongue in cheek, Morellet claimed that Franklin supported America's independence so as to free himself from the need to drink English tea and eat inferior English food, and to allow himself the opportunity to enjoy more French champagne. The song ended with a toast readers of *French Philadelphia* are invited to join: "Le verre en main, chantons notre Benjamin!" (Glass in hand, let's hear it for our Benjamin!)

INTRODUCTION

William Penn's "City of Brotherly Love," his "Holy Experiment," his "Greene Countrie Towne," has gone through many phases since its founder first began to realize his dream of a society built on religious tolerance in 1682. Within a century, Philadelphia became the most cosmopolitan city of the Americas, the second-largest urban center in the English-speaking world (after London), the "Cradle of Liberty," and the capital of the new nation. In another hundred years, Philadelphia was the main engine of the Industrial Revolution in America and the fourth largest city on the planet, with a population of some 600,000 by 1880. During the 20th century, its population at least tripled once more before suburbanization pulled some of its residents beyond city limits. It is today a thriving post-industrial center for health services, higher education, and high-tech industry, while remaining a city rich in history, culture, and trade. Some four million people live in the greater metropolitan area.

Throughout the centuries, France and the French have played an important role in Philadelphia's development. In the early years, the magnet was the religious and political freedoms available here. After the revocation of the Edict of Nantes (1685), many groups of Huguenots, as the French followers of Calvin were known, came to Pennsylvania to be able to worship as they pleased. Then for decades, starting in the mid-eighteenth century, Philadelphia received many thousands of French people. Refugees came, following the cession of all of Canada to the British, in the aftermath of the expulsion of the French Acadians from what became Nova Scotia (1755). Statesmen, adventurers, and soldiers arrived throughout the period of the War of Independence (1776–1783), thanks to France's support of the would-be new nation. With the French Revolution (1789), the upheaval that followed in the French West Indies, and the aftermath of Waterloo (1815), Philadelphia received many thousands more French people uprooted from their homelands.

Their cultural, social, political, and economic impact left deep impressions on Penn's fundamentally English town.

Since then, though their relative numbers have declined, more French people have settled here. So, in the last decades of the 20th century, did many refugees from such Francophone countries as Cambodia, Laos and Viet Nam, as well as Haitians seeking an escape from political and social unrest. With the help of enthusiastic Francophiles, they have kept alive and enriched the cultural impact that the early settlers and visitors made on the Quaker City.

French institutions abound here today: the French-American Chamber of Commerce of Philadelphia, with more than 500 members, is one of the most important binational chambers of commerce in the region. The presence for more than a century of the Alliance Française de Philadelphie is testimony both to its role in the diffusion of French culture, language, and literature, and to the way in which it has nourished and encouraged Franco-American friendship by adapting to the tradition, direction and special style of Philadelphia.

THE FRENCH IN PHILADELPHIA: HIGHLIGHTS

At the birth of the United States of America, the Franco-American connection was both strong and unique, thanks to the fact that France became the emerging nation's first ally in its war of independence from Britain. Philadelphia's role in forging this invaluable tie was critical. The alliance was brought into being above all because of the efforts of this city's leading citizen, Benjamin Franklin. Sent to Paris in 1776 by the Continental Congress, Franklin lived there throughout the rest of the war, where he was hailed as one of the greatest figures of his age. Franklin returned France's admiration by becoming a thorough Francophile and a leading figure in Parisian social and intellectual circles. He was chiefly responsible for securing critical financial assistance for the American effort from the government of Louis XVI, and for the Treaty of Paris, which officially ended the war and recognized America's independence from Great Britain in 1783.

Le Docteur Franklin couronné par la Liberté
Courtesy of the
Athenæum of Philadelphia.

As the nation's capital, Philadelphia was host to the first French emissaries who arrived early in the war to further the cause of American independence. In 1775, the first secret emissary of France to the Congress in Philadelphia was the chevalier Julien-Alexandre Achard de Bonvouloir et Loyauté. The chevalier arrived in Philadelphia with a year-old commission as a lieutenant, which suggested he was an officer no longer on active duty. He had the assistance of Francis Daymon, a Frenchman established in Philadelphia, who was the friend of a merchant in Saint-Domingue (today's Haiti) known to the chevalier from his earlier voyage to the West Indies. Daymon, a Parisian by birth who had emigrated to America, was by then a librarian for the Library Company of Philadelphia. He had just been chosen as a secretary to the Congress. Thanks to Daymon, the chevalier had several meetings with Benjamin Franklin, John Jay, John Dickinson, and others at Carpenters' Hall. These meetings were held at night so as not to attract the attention of British agents, the Americans taking care to arrive one by one. Reports on these meetings sent by Bonvouloir to the comte de Vergennes, the French foreign minister, opened the way for Franco-American negotiations.

Later, there came to America the dashing young marquis de Lafayette, who was encouraged by Franklin in his effort to join the struggle at a time when France was still officially neutral. Lafayette soon fought with distinction by Washington's side. He contributed substantially to the American cause and became the first non-native hero of the new nation. In 1824, Lafayette returned to a tumultuous welcome in the United States. During that visit, he attended the rededication of Philadelphia's State House, and it was Lafayette who first named it America's "Hall of Independence" [see Independence Park & Penn's Landing].

Among temporary visitors displaced from France by the French Revolution was Charles-Maurice de Talleyrand (1754–1838), who lived in a small apartment on North 3rd Street during much of 1794 through 1796. The cleric-turned-statesman was said to have scandalized Quaker Philadelphia—which reportedly bored him—by openly consorting with a beautiful young Creole woman from Saint-Domingue. Stories conflict as to whether it was she, or a poor woman of Philadelphia, who was the mother of his child. Yet it was none other than a Philadelphia Quaker who later reported that this "notorious libertine" nonetheless supported mother and child through the years after he returned to Napoleonic France and became one of the most influential public figures in Europe.[1]

At about the time Benjamin Franklin left Philadelphia for France, a young seaman from Bordeaux, Stephen (Étienne) Girard (1750–1831), landed unexpectedly in Philadelphia. A

---

[1] Thomas P. Cope, an unpublished diary, 1847.

cabin boy at fourteen and the captain of his vessel by 1776, he found his way into New York blocked by a British blockade of the harbor; he reversed course and sailed up the Delaware River instead, to dock in Philadelphia. This twenty-six-year-old looked about the bustling city and decided to settle down here. He sold his ship and the interest in his cargo and opened a small business on Philadelphia's Water Street (today's Columbus Boulevard). Over the next decades, he grew wealthy. He acquired a fleet of beautiful clipper ships that engaged in world-wide trade, naming some of them for *philosophes* of the French Enlightenment: Montesquieu, Rousseau, Voltaire. Shrewd investments in land and mines increased his fortune. Mean-while, he became a highly successful banker, almost single-handedly financing the War of 1812. In 1816, he subscribed a huge amount to underwrite the Second Bank of the United States.

Stephen Girard

Courtesy of the Athenæum of Philadelphia.

In 1793, during one of the terrible yellow fever epidemics that swept through Philadel-phia, Girard led the effort to organize and improve hospital care for the sick. Throughout the rest of his life, his chari-table work grew along with his fortune; at his death in 1831, he was the wealthiest man in the country. The results of his philanthropy are felt to the present day. One of his major bequests created Girard Col-lege, which opened its doors in 1848 to fatherless boys between the ages of ten and eighteen. The school is now a co-educational boarding school whose magnificent Founder's Hall houses Girard's tomb, as well as a collection of his personal effects [see Benjamin Franklin Parkway for details]. Girard also left much property to the city of Philadelphia.

The slave rebellion on Saint-Domingue in 1795 brought a flood of newly indigent French and Creole refugees to Philadel-phia. A M(onsieur) Collot, who may have been among them, seems to have been the first in a successful line of ice cream makers of African descent in the city. He advertised in Philadelphia newspapers that he had moved his business into large quarters where he would continue to make ice cream "in all the perfection of the true Italian mode." Another Frenchman compared Collot's ice cream favorably to that of the Palais Royal in Paris. A few years earlier, Thomas Jefferson, an ardent Francophile, was living in Philadelphia as Secretary of State of the United States. He wrote to the American envoy in Paris in 1791, at the height of the French Revolution, requesting a shipment of fifty vanilla pods to make his favorite ice cream.

The debacle that followed Napoléon's defeat at Waterloo brought a wave of French refugees to America. Among them was a young soldier, Michael (Michel) Bouvier, from Pont-Saint-Esprit in the Rhône valley. A skilled cabinet-maker, he first settled in New York; two years later, he came to Philadelphia. He established a furniture business on South 2nd Street, prospered, married in 1822, and became an American citizen. After his first wife died, he remarried and fathered ten children while becoming ever more prosperous as the result of hard work, judicious investments, and the patronage of Stephen Girard and Joseph Bonaparte. Devoutly Catholic, Bouvier and his family were known for their charity; Michael was a long-time director, then president (1869-1874), of the French Benevolent Society, which for two centuries provided "moral or financial assistance to those of French descent" in Philadelphia. One of his daughters became a nun and another, Emma Bouvier Drexel, became the step-mother of Katherine Drexel, who was canonized by Pope John Paul II in 2000. The great-great granddaughter of Michael and Louise Bouvier, Jacqueline Bouvier Kennedy, became first lady of the United States when her husband was inaugurated as President in 1961 [see Society Hill for more on the Bouvier family].

William Penn had laid out his model city with streets on a grid pattern, the lowest-numbered streets starting at the Delaware and running north and south across the narrow waist of land to the Schuylkill River, some two miles to the west. These were (and still are) crossed by east-west streets, mostly given the names of local trees: Chestnut, Walnut, Locust, Spruce, Pine. Penn's original plan formed a rough quadrant, in each of whose four corners was laid out a public park-like square, with a fifth, Center Square, more or less in the middle. It was at Center Square where the wide north-south Broad Street intersected with the east-west axis, High (now Market) Street. Penn's plan remains unchanged to the present, although Center Square has been, since the 1870s, the site of Philadelphia's City Hall, the largest public building in America when it was constructed.

Built in the French Renaissance or Second Empire style, City Hall bears more than a little resemblance to its counterpart, the Hôtel de Ville in Paris. It forms the southeastern anchor of a grand boulevard, the Benjamin Franklin Parkway, which was designed early in the 20th century and brought to completion by two French architects, Paul-Philippe Cret and Jacques Gréber. The Parkway created a diagonal slash across Penn's grid to link the center of the city with Fairmount Park—the largest urban park in the world—which ambles along both banks of the Schuylkill River and the Wissahickon Creek to Philadelphia's northwestern limits. What is immediately apparent about the Parkway is its resemblance to Paris's Avenue des Champs-Elysées. Roughly halfway along its route toward the Philadelphia Museum of Art and the entrance to Fairmount Park, Penn's Northwest Square was transformed into Logan Circle, now the site of the magnificent Swann Fountain. Just to the north stand the Philadelphia Free Library and the Municipal Court, twin buildings modeled after the Marine Ministry and the Hôtel de Crillon in Paris. Taken as a whole, then, this space is Philadelphia's Place de la Concorde. There are many more signs of French, and especially Parisian, influence in art and architecture of this area as well [see Benjamin Franklin Parkway for more].

In the near-century since the completion of the Parkway, the impact of French people and culture on Philadelphia has continued. In the 1960s, a young Frenchman, Georges Perrier, arrived in Philadelphia as head chef of La Panetière restaurant. Three years later, he created what would become his durable five-star restaurant, **Le Bec-Fin** (below), still regarded, as it has been for decades, as one of the nation's finest. Perrier's superb cuisine influenced the creation of other notable bistros, cafés, and restaurants in Philadelphia, which began a booming restaurant renaissance in the 1970s that continues to the present. Many of these establishments naturally owe much to the French

tradition, whether in its purest culinary form or via fusion with other cuisines, such as those of the Orient. Today, any promenade along Philadelphia's "Restaurant Row" near Rittenhouse Square—particularly in summer when diners revel at sidewalk restaurants with names like Rouge, Bleu, Le Jardin, Brasserie Perrier, and others—reveals the city's love affair with French cuisine. The Gallic influence is so great here that the neighborhood is now officially designated as Philadelphia's "French Quarter." Nor are French restaurants confined to this neighborhood, but are sprinkled liberally throughout the city. In relation to its size, there are reportedly more French-inspired eating places in Philadelphia than in any other American city [see Rittenhouse Square & Delancy Place for more].

In 2004, the people of Normandy had a replica of Philadelphia's Liberty Bell made to commemorate the 60th anniversary of the Allies' D-Day invasion of Normandy that led to the liberation of France from Nazi occupation. The next summer, in 2005, that bell was brought to Philadelphia. Starting with the nation's Independence Day celebration on the 4th of July, it was displayed first at the National Constitution Center, then on the Battleship New Jersey, which is permanently anchored on the Camden, New Jersey shore of the Delaware River, across from Philadelphia. Sponsors of the Normandy Liberty Bell hope to make it the centerpiece of a new monument at the American Cemetery above Omaha Beach in Normandy. The original bell's clear E-flat has not been heard since 1846 because of its famous, irreparable crack. But thanks to this gift from France, twenty-first-century Americans were able to hear how the original bell sounded. The bell became only the latest, tangible expression of the centuries-old bond connecting France with Philadelphia.

TWO EIGHTEENTH-CENTURY REPORTERS

Today's visitors to Philadelphia can see and even recapture some of the ambience in which, two centuries ago, French refugees, exiles, émigrés and statesmen lived, worked and (in many cases) awaited the end of the revolution in France before returning home or settling here. Of those early visitors and settlers, two keen and observant Frenchmen wrote journals which provide marvelous glimpses of life in Philadelphia as they experienced it in the late 18th century.

François-Jean de Beauvoir, chevalier de Chastellux (1734–1788) was both a professional soldier and a man of letters, "as clever with the pen as with the sword." His *Travels in America (Voyages de M. le marquis de Chastellux dans l'Amérique septentrionale dans les années 1780, 1781, et 1782)* is not a soldier's report on military matters, but rather a narrative of his journeys when not on active duty.

The marquis came from a noble family whose sons traditionally made careers in the army. The young chevalier de Chastellux did likewise. He accompanied the French Expeditionary Forces to America as one of the three major-generals ranking just below the comte de Rochambeau, commanding general of the 6,000 French regulars. Chastellux was present at the decisive, final battle of Yorktown, Virginia, in 1781, which brought Cornwallis's surrender and independence for America. His knowledge of English made him an intermediary between the French and American officials so that he became known as the diplomat of Rochambeau's army. Esteemed by Washington and the many Americans he met, Chastellux was elected in 1781 a member of the American Philosophical Society. His portrait, one of many done by the American painter Charles Willson Peale, is on display at the Second Bank of the United States [for details, see Independence Park and Penn's Landing].

Médéric-Louis-Elie Moreau de Saint-Méry (1750–1819), who was described as "tall, well proportioned, of pleasing presence and ready wit," was born at Fort-Royal, Martinique, French West Indies, on January 13, 1750. After having succeeded brilliantly in law studies in Paris, he settled in Santo Domingo, where he practiced and began the great collection of laws for which he was renowned during his lifetime. In Paris again from 1784 to 1790, he played a role as champion of the French Revolution. He is credited with having proposed his friend Lafayette as commander for the guard of Paris. An ardent proponent of reform, he was firmly opposed to lawlessness, thus insuring the hostility of the radical elements. With the rise of Robespierre, he had to flee Paris.

At Le Havre, Moreau and his family boarded a ship bound for New York. They landed in Norfolk, Virginia, after a stormy 119-day voyage, and finally reached New York via New Castle, Wilmington and Philadelphia—to which the family returned after a few months. Here, Moreau de Saint-Méry established a book and printing shop. As his scholarly renown grew, he, too, was elected a member of the American Philosophical Society. Shortly before returning to France in 1798, Moreau had the pleasure of greeting the refugee son of Lafayette, who had recently been freed from an Austrian prison by Napoléon. In France, Moreau de Saint-Méry resumed a notable career. He died there in January, 1819.

One of the charms of Philadelphia today is that some of its blocks, streets, and whole neighborhoods are little changed from the time Chastellux and Moreau de Saint-Méry were living here.

Old St. Joseph's Church, Willings Alley

Even while Philadelphia has grown and changed over the three-plus centuries since its creation, it has also conserved much of its past—more, in fact, than that of any other American city of comparable size. Because there was space for the city to grow, many of the original streets and neighborhoods of the town Penn and, two generations later, Franklin knew were left largely untouched through succeeding centuries. In the course of the 19th century, the well-to-do built their mansions ever farther from the center, inventing whole communities as the Pennsylvania

Railroad made such development practicable along its elite Main Line to the west of the city. Meanwhile, some older neighborhoods declined, and some became shabby before they were rescued and renovated in the years beginning after World War II. Today, whole districts in and around Center City (Philadelphians' term for the area corresponding roughly to Penn's original boundaries) are scrubbed, restored, and vibrant. Increasing numbers of residents have settled in these neighborhoods very close to, and sometimes in, the commercial center, creating districts teeming with social life, as they did in the days when all of Philadelphia was contained here. These neighborhoods of Center City can easily be toured on foot.

Now Philadelphia's downtown is pierced with the kinds of steel-and-glass skyscrapers that are characteristic of all modern metropolises. Some of these buildings—such as the pointed towers of Liberty Place with the blue-tinted ziggurats of their capped roofs; the PSFS building (now Loew's Hotel), which was the nation's first great Bauhaus structure; or the glittering planes of the cubist sculpture that constitutes the Cira Center—make dramatic architectural statements and a distinctive skyline for the city.

For Philadelphians, however, it is probably still the nineteenth-century tower of City Hall that creates the most recognizable and beloved profile from afar. Standing at the pinnacle of its graceful upward-sweeping roof is a thirty-seven-foot bronze statue of Pennsylvania's founder, William Penn. It was Penn's grand plan for a city built on principles of peace and toleration that made Philadelphia such a beacon of enlightenment in its early years. This likeness of Pennsylvania's founder was created by Alexander Milne Calder in the 1870s. Fittingly, it would tower over the city Penn dreamed into being from the very center of his original plan for Philadelphia, which extended from the Delaware to the Schuylkill Rivers, and from today's South Street to Vine Street on the north. Penn's use of a grid pattern for his new city, with streets that crossed each other at regular, right-angled intervals, was such a model of clarity and common sense that it soon became standard for most of the new towns and cities of America.

INDEPENDENCE PARK & PENN'S LANDING

Most visitors to Philadelphia today are drawn first to the most famous of our American historical monuments. Independence Hall, on Chestnut between 5th and 6th Streets, is the elegant and modest building where the two great documents of American liberty and self-government, the Declaration of Independence and the Constitution of the United States, were framed and adopted. It was here, in 1775, that George Washington received his commission as commander of the armies that would attempt to assert the independence of Britain's thirteen North American colonies from the imperial government in London. It was here, on a hot July day in 1776, that the representatives of these same colonies would pledge their lives, their fortunes and their sacred honor to achieving that independence. It was also here, in 1787, that the victorious Washington presided over the convention that wrote a constitution for the newly independent United States, still struggling with the effort to act with strength and unity while preserving the liberties for which the Americans had fought.

But there is even more to the history of this American shrine. From the time it was built in the 1730s to house the colonial government of Pennsylvania through the period ending in 1812, when Philadelphia served as the capital of the Commonwealth of Pennsylvania, this building was officially Pennsylvania's State House. Meanwhile, from 1790 to 1800, Philadelphia was the infant nation's capital, and both the United States Congress and Supreme Court met in the State House complex. After the national capital moved to the new District of Columbia and the capital of the Commonwealth was moved to Harrisburg, these buildings were home to Philadelphia's city government. So, one of the distinctions of Independence Hall and its adjoining buildings—Old City Hall to the east and Congress Hall on the west—is that this is the only site in America that has been the official seat of colonial, city, state and Federal governments.

Today, Independence Hall and its surrounding area are administered by the National Park Service of the United States, and visits are by guided tour. The Liberty Bell, which for some two centuries hung in the Independence Hall bell tower, is now located in a new pavilion directly across Chestnut Street from Congress Hall. One block further north, at the corner of 6th and Market Streets, the Independence Visitor Center provides a full array of information regarding sites to visit in Independence Park, Philadelphia and the surrounding area. At the northern end of Independence Mall, between Arch and Race, 5th and 6th Streets, the National Constitution Center provides a dramatic setting in which to learn about the importance of the Constitution of the United States through film presentations, pictorial exhibits and informative programs. Life-size bronze statues of each of the Constitution's founders are one exhibit. (For information on all sites in Independence National Historical Park, phone 215-597-8974, or go to www.nps.gov/inde).

Immediately in front of **Independence Hall**'s central entrance stands a splendid bronze statue of **George Washington** (photo, left) by the noted French sculptor Alexis Bailly. This is a copy of the original marble sculpture placed here in 1869 and later removed to City Hall for its protection.

Inside Independence Hall, the great assembly room looks almost exactly as it did on those occasions in the late 18th century when two documents drafted here would guide the future destiny of the United States. The Declaration of Independence and the Constitution are among the finest achievements of the Age of Enlightenment. Their authors were steeped in the ideas of the leading thinkers of the period, both French and English, and they incorporated many of them into these sets of principles and actions for a novel form of government.

Among the French *philosophes* with the greatest influence on the American founders were Voltaire (1694-1778), with his skepticism about traditional authority; Rousseau (1712-1778), and his emphasis on egalitarianism; Condorcet (1743-1794), whose progressive view of history was shared by many of the founders; and, above all, Montesquieu (1689-1755), whose *Esprit des lois* (1748) launched the idea of tripartite government, each checking and balancing the other. Montesquieu's work was read and studied by Thomas Jefferson and James Madison—the two most important contributors to the Declaration and the Constitution respectively—

11

and by many others involved in drafting these works. Washington had made himself familiar with the reasoning of Montesquieu as well. In very important respects, Montesquieu's influence was fundamental to the shape and content of the new American institutions of government.

Moreau de Saint-Méry provides an eyewitness account of an occasion when President Washington attended a meeting with Congress at these buildings on Chestnut Street:

> Promptly at noon on the nineteenth of September, 1794, Washington arrived alone in a carriage drawn by four horses. His three servants and his coachman wore white liveries with red collars and cuffs. [. . .]
>
> Seven high constables with white wands walked before the carriage and in front of them fourteen constables.
>
> Washington was dressed in black, his hair in a bag (snood), a turned up hat and sword. He did not wear his hat, nor did anyone else. There was no applause on the President's arrival or departure. The silence which reigns in the galleries of Congress deserves the highest praise.[2]

Washington presumably had arrived from his rented house a mere block away, at the corner of 6th and Market Streets. That early Executive Mansion was demolished during the 19th century, but a plaque near the Liberty Bell pavilion allows visitors to see where it stood.

The first floor of Congress Hall held the House of Representatives while the Senate chamber occupied the second floor during the decade when Philadelphia served as the nation's capital. In a room adjacent to the Senate, two portraits of Louis XVI and of Marie-Antoinette are displayed. These are copies of two portraits presented to the American government in honor of the Franco-American alliance of 1778. They were moved to Washington, DC when that new city, carved from the wilderness, became the nation's capital. During the War of 1812, the building in Washington in which they hung was burned by the British and the portraits were destroyed. On May 19, 1976, Philadelphia was honored by the visit

---

[2] *Moreau de Saint-Méry's American Journey 1793-1798*, translated and edited by Kenneth Roberts and Anna M. Roberts (Garden City, New York: Doubleday & Company, 1947) 349-350.

of the President of the French Republic, Valéry Giscard d'Estaing, and his wife. In a ceremony on Independence Mall, President Giscard presented these two copies of the originals.

During the 19th century, state receptions were held in the State House, often in the long gallery on the second floor. One of the most brilliant was given in honor of the marquis de Lafayette when he revisited the United States in 1824-25.

On the northwest corner of 6th and Chestnut Streets, across from the Liberty Bell pavilion, stood the French Legation and the residence of its ministers to the young republic (a red brick bank building now stands on part of the site). This was John Dickinson's town house, which was surrounded by a garden that extended the entire block between 6th and 7th Streets. It was rented, first, to the chevalier Conrad-Alexandre Gérard and, following his retirement, to the marquis de la Luzerne, both of whom represented the government of Louis XVI.

Gérard (1729-1790) had occupied a number of posts in Europe before coming to the United States. He was a confidante of the French Foreign Minister, the comte de Vergennes, and was the chief negotiator on the French side for the treaty of alliance with America. He lobbied vigorously to become the first envoy of his country to the United States and, while here, was deeply engaged in American affairs. His correspondence with Vergennes reveals much about the political climate and the social life of the growing nation. In one letter, he tells of the honor of being elected to membership in the American Philosophical Society; in another, he reports an interview with French-born Anthony (Antoine) Benezet, the Quaker philanthropist. In 1779, when Gérard was obliged to return to France because of ill health, his services were extolled in the Pennsylvania Gazette.

The marquis de la Luzerne (1741-1791) resided in Philadelphia as France's minister from 1779 to 1783. He was an officer, an affable host, and a consummate diplomat who seems to have respected all of his host country's customs no matter how odd they may have seemed to him. He, too, was elected a member of the American Philosophical Society.

It was during the marquis de la Luzerne's term that the news was brought to the legation of the arrival in Philadelphia of French troops and of the French ships in Chesapeake Bay. The soldiers were under the command of Jean-Baptiste de Vimeur, comte de Rochambeau (1725-1807), who had already had a brilliant military

13

career before coming to America. Early in 1781, the French troops were encamped in Newport, Rhode Island, where they had remained inactive for many months. Finally, on June 10, 1781, the first divisions marched out on their way to join Washington on the Hudson River above New York City. After having marched 548 miles in thirty-seven days, the troops, 6,000 strong, arrived in Philadelphia on September 3. About a mile from town they halted, brushed and chalked their white uniforms, and trimmed their grenadier hats with white and rose-colored plumes. The abbé Robin, regimental chaplain, gave this account:

> The arrival of the French army at Philadelphia was more like a triumph than simply a passing through the place. They marched through the town, up Chestnut Street to Center Square where they camped [see the bronze plaque at the west entrance to the courtyard of City Hall]; with military music playing before them, which is always particularly pleasing to the Americans; the streets were crowded with people, and the ladies appeared at the windows in their most brilliant attire. All Philadelphia was astonished to see people who had endured the fatigue of a long journey so ruddy and handsome, and even wondered that there could be Frenchmen of so genteel an appearance![3]

The commander of the French ships then in the Chesapeake was François-Joseph-Paul, comte de Grasse (1722–1788). He was born in Provence, where there was great enthusiasm for the American cause, and at a young age took service in the galleys of the Order of Malta. In 1740, he entered the French service, and in 1781, shortly after France and the United States joined forces in the Revolutionary War, he was dispatched to America as commander.

When Washington and Rochambeau determined to march to Virginia and join forces with Lafayette's army against Cornwallis, Washington requested the cooperation of the comte de Grasse's fleet, which therefore sailed from the West Indies to the Chesapeake. The abbé Robin reported how the news of the fleet's arrival came to Philadelphia. During a gala dinner given by Luzerne for the just-arrived French officers and guests, "[. . .] an express arrived: a disquieting silence immediately seized every guest [. . .] . Our eyes

---

[3] Abbé Robin, *Nouveau voyage dans l'Amérique septentrionale, en l'année 1781; et campagne de l'armée de M. le comte de Rochambeau.* (Philadelphie : et se trouve à Paris, Chez Moutard, 1782) Passage translated by Annette H. Emgarth.

were fixed upon the chevalier de la Luzerne, everyone endeavoring to guess what the message would turn out to be. 'Thirty-six ships of the line,' said he, 'commanded by Monsieur le comte de Grasse, have arrived in Chesapeake Bay, and three thousand men have landed and opened a communication with the marquis de Lafayette.' Joy and good humor immediately resumed their place on every countenance."

The French ships, by effectively blocking the English on the nearby peninsula, made possible their defeat at Yorktown. That most decisive battle, which brought the surrender of the British army on October 19, 1781, and the end of the military conflict, was itself the result of remarkable cooperation and coordination. Some 16,000 men composed of three armies—those of Washington, Rochambeau, and Lafayette—had converged over 1,600 miles to engage in the three-week siege that brought about the British defeat. From the allied side, cries of « *Vive le Roi !* » alternated with those of "God and liberty!" as word of the British capitulation spread.

After Cornwallis's surrender, the comte de Grasse returned to the West Indies where he captured the island of St. Kitts in January 1782. In April, however, he was defeated by the British Admiral Rodney and taken prisoner. He died in Paris on January 11, 1788. He had been a naval officer of great merit—a big, hot-tempered man, standing six feet two on ordinary days, but, according to his sailors, six feet six on battle days!

General Lafayette by François Casanova. Courtesy of the Athenæum of Philadelphia.

Then there was Lafayette: Marie-Joseph-Gilbert-Paul-Yves-Roche-Gilbert du Motier, marquis de Lafayette (1757-1834), who became truly legendary among the numerous French friends of the United States during its earliest years. He first sailed for America, at the age of nineteen, from the port of Pasjes in the Spanish Basque country. In Paris, Franklin enthusiastically encouraged his mission, which Lafayette undertook against the wishes of his own rich and influential family. Already a professional soldier and a devoted husband and soon-to-be father, he was a fearless and impulsive young idealist, determined to join the fight for liberty. Washington, who recognized worth and talent when he saw them, quickly appreciated Lafayette's abilities. Soon he was commissioned a major-general in the Continental army. His real concern for the enlisted soldiers with whom he fought at Brandywine where he was wounded, at Monmouth, and at Yorktown endeared him to his men.

In May, 1778, his escape with his troops from the British at Barren Hill—today renamed Lafayette Hill—in the Conshohocken-Plymouth-Whitemarsh area just outside Philadelphia was a remarkable maneuver worthy of the most seasoned soldier. When he returned to America some forty-six years later in 1824-25, Lafayette retraced his travels and visited friends. While in Philadelphia, wishing to see again the famous escape route he had taken to rejoin Washington at Valley Forge, he was accompanied by soldiers and citizen groups along the Germantown Pike to Barren Hill [see Germantown & Chestnut Hill].

During the War of Independence, Lafayette was feted socially wherever he went. In Philadelphia, he frequently visited the Samuel Powels [the Powel House, at 244 S. 3rd Street, is open to the public], went to Mass with Rochambeau and the comte de Grasse at St. Joseph's Church [in Willing's Alley below Walnut near 4th Street—see photo on page 8], and attended services at Christ Church [at Second and Market Streets]. In 1781, he was elected a member of the American Philosophical Society.

Three days following Cornwallis's surrender at Yorktown, Queen Marie-Antoinette of France gave birth to an heir to the throne. The happy event was officially announced the following spring to the Congress of the United States by the French Minister, the marquis de la Luzerne. Several months later, in August, 1782, the marquis hosted a lavish party in honor of the infant dauphin, Louis Joseph, at his rented house between 6th and 7th Streets on Chestnut. In a letter written the next day, Dr. Benjamin Rush, a renowned Philadelphia physician, had this to say:

> Hundreds crowded daily to see a large frame building he had erected on one side of his house. This building, which was sixty feet in front and forty feet deep, was supported by large painted pillars and was open all round. The ceiling was decorated [. . .] . The garden [. . .] was cut into walks and divided with cedar and

pine branches into artificial groves [. . .] . For ten days before the entertainment, nothing else was talked of in our city.[4]

The large frame building, by the way, had been designed by Pierre L'Enfant, an engineer in Rochambeau's army, who would become famous in America a few years later as the planner of the new Federal capital city, Washington, DC.

The morning of the event was ushered in by a corps of hair-dressers occupying the place of the city watchmen. Many ladies were obliged to have their heads dressed between four and six o'clock in the morning, so great was the demand. When the long-awaited evening arrived, according to Dr. Rush:

> The chevalier de la Luzerne appeared with all the splendor of the Minister and all the politeness of the gentleman. He walked along the tables and addressed himself in particular to every lady. The supper was a cold collection, simple, frugal and elegant and handsomely set off with a dessert consisting of cakes and all the fruits of the season.

> General and Mrs. Washington, comte de Rochambeau, the marquis de Chastellux, Robert Morris, John Dickinson, General Thomas Mifflin and a host of distinguished men and women were there while an Indian chief or two lent variety to the scene—especially so when a Chief in his savage habits and the comte de Rochambeau in his expensive and splendid uniform talked with each other as if they had been the subjects of the same government, generals in the same army, and the partakers of the same blessings of civilized life.

> A most unique feature of the entertainment was an apartment fitted up by the thoughtful host for the reception of those Quaker ladies whose principles would not permit them to join in the gaiety, but who watched the dancers through a gauze curtain! This little attention to the curiosity of these ladies marks in the strongest manner the Minister's desire to please everybody.[5]

America's gratitude for the French presence in Philadelphia at the time of the Revolution is readily seen in the Second Bank of the United States, on Chestnut between 4th and 5th Streets. Now a Revolutionary-era portrait gallery, this serene Greek Revival temple

---

[4] Agnès Repplier paraphrases Benjamin Rush's description in *Philadelphia: The Place and the People.* (New York: Macmillan, 1898) 261-263.

[5] Repplier 261-263.

houses hundreds of life portraits of those who were important in the American cause. Most of the paintings were done by the great eighteenth-century Philadelphia artist, Charles Willson Peale, who made it his goal to capture on canvas as many of his notable contemporaries as possible. These were displayed during Peale's lifetime in his museum, on the second floor of Independence Hall.

In this collection are nine Frenchmen who helped the Americans achieve their independence. Lafayette is represented with two fine portraits: the one by Peale is bust-sized and shows him as a reddish-haired young man; the other, by the younger Philadelphia artist Thomas Sully, is a full-length portrait of Lafayette as he appeared on his return visit to America when he was sixty-seven years old. Peale depicted Gérard in a full-length portrait with Independence Hall in the background. Of the other Peale portraits, those of Rochambeau and Chastellux are of particular interest. Also on display are portraits of the following:

> **Louis le Begne de Presle, Duportail** (1743–1802), who commanded the rebuilding of forts along the Delaware River and the defenses at West Point, later organizing the Valley Forge encampment;
> **Louis-Antoine-Jean-Baptiste, chevalier de Cambray-Digny** (1751–1822), who served the Continental army in the engineering corps;
> **Jean-Baptiste, chevalier de Ternant** (1751–1816), who served in Washington's army throughout the Revolution, then returned in 1791 as France's foreign minister;
> **Constantin-François Chasseboeuf, comte de Volney** (1757–1820), a scientist and scholar, who toured the United States over the course of three years in the mid-1790s, when he was elected to the American Philosophical Society;
> **Pierre-François, comte de Réal** (1757–1807), a friend and confidante of Joseph Bonaparte, whom he briefly joined in Philadelphia during Bonaparte's exile here in 1815.

In the next block east of the Second Bank, nothing now remains of the path once taken by Dock Creek (although the path of the creek, long ago drained, is apparent in that of Dock Street, to the southeast). Early in the 18th century, Dock Creek cut across Chestnut between 3rd and 4th Streets, and a bridge had been built over it. At the head of the bridge there stood, circa 1734, the home of Anthony Benezet (1713-1784), a well-known Quaker philanthropist.

were fixed upon the chevalier de la Luzerne, everyone endeavoring to guess what the message would turn out to be. 'Thirty-six ships of the line,' said he, 'commanded by Monsieur le comte de Grasse, have arrived in Chesapeake Bay, and three thousand men have landed and opened a communication with the marquis de Lafayette.' Joy and good humor immediately resumed their place on every countenance."

The French ships, by effectively blocking the English on the nearby peninsula, made possible their defeat at Yorktown. That most decisive battle, which brought the surrender of the British army on October 19, 1781, and the end of the military conflict, was itself the result of remarkable cooperation and coordination. Some 16,000 men composed of three armies—those of Washington, Rochambeau, and Lafayette—had converged over 1,600 miles to engage in the three-week siege that brought about the British defeat. From the allied side, cries of « *Vive le Roi !* » alternated with those of "God and liberty!" as word of the British capitulation spread.

After Cornwallis's surrender, the comte de Grasse returned to the West Indies where he captured the island of St. Kitts in January 1782. In April, however, he was defeated by the British Admiral Rodney and taken prisoner. He died in Paris on January 11, 1788. He had been a naval officer of great merit—a big, hot-tempered man, standing six feet two on ordinary days, but, according to his sailors, six feet six on battle days!

General Lafayette by François Casanova. Courtesy of the Athenæum of Philadelphia.

Then there was Lafayette: Marie-Joseph-Gilbert-Paul-Yves-Roche-Gilbert du Motier, marquis de Lafayette (1757–1834), who became truly legendary among the numerous French friends of the United States during its earliest years. He first sailed for America, at the age of nineteen, from the port of Pasjes in the Spanish Basque country. In Paris, Franklin enthusiastically encouraged his mission, which Lafayette undertook against the wishes of his own rich and influential family. Already a professional

15

soldier and a devoted husband and soon-to-be father, he was a fearless and impulsive young idealist, determined to join the fight for liberty. Washington, who recognized worth and talent when he saw them, quickly appreciated Lafayette's abilities. Soon he was commissioned a major-general in the Continental army. His real concern for the enlisted soldiers with whom he fought at Brandy-wine where he was wounded, at Monmouth, and at Yorktown endeared him to his men.

In May, 1778, his escape with his troops from the British at Barren Hill—today renamed Lafayette Hill—in the Conshohocken-Plymouth-Whitemarsh area just outside Philadelphia was a remarkable maneuver worthy of the most seasoned soldier. When he returned to America some forty-six years later in 1824–25, Lafayette retraced his travels and visited friends. While in Philadelphia, wishing to see again the famous escape route he had taken to rejoin Washington at Valley Forge, he was accompanied by soldiers and citizen groups along the Germantown Pike to Barren Hill [see Germantown & Chestnut Hill].

During the War of Independence, Lafayette was feted socially wherever he went. In Philadelphia, he frequently visited the Samuel Powels [the Powel House, at 244 S. 3rd Street, is open to the public], went to Mass with Rochambeau and the comte de Grasse at St. Joseph's Church [in Willing's Alley below Walnut near 4th Street—see photo on page 8], and attended services at Christ Church [at Second and Market Streets]. In 1781, he was elected a member of the American Philosophical Society.

Three days following Cornwallis's surrender at Yorktown, Queen Marie-Antoinette of France gave birth to an heir to the throne. The happy event was officially announced the following spring to the Congress of the United States by the French Minister, the marquis de la Luzerne. Several months later, in August, 1782, the marquis hosted a lavish party in honor of the infant dauphin, Louis Joseph, at his rented house between 6th and 7th Streets on Chestnut. In a letter written the next day, Dr. Benjamin Rush, a renowned Philadelphia physician, had this to say:

> Hundreds crowded daily to see a large frame building he had erected on one side of his house. This building, which was sixty feet in front and forty feet deep, was supported by large painted pillars and was open all round. The ceiling was decorated [. . .] . The garden [. . .] was cut into walks and divided with cedar and

(Lafayette's brother-in-law); the duc d'Orléans (future King Louis-Philippe); la Rochefoucauld-Liancourt, whose much-read work *On the Prisons of Philadelphia by An* [sic] *European* (1796) in English and in French bore the pressmark of "Moreau de St. Méry, Printer and Bookseller"; and Charles-Maurice de Talleyrand-Périgord, who was the most assiduous visitor of all.

From Moreau's printing press, there came many well-known works of various authors—as well as some of his own, a daily newspaper, and even a school text. One diary entry says, "It was during 1797 that I decided to have my outline of science translated into English and published in this language. [. . .] This edition was quickly exhausted because American schools adopted it for their teaching." While in Philadelphia, Moreau also was honored by the American Philosophical Society, which elected him a resident member, thus adding to several honorary titles bestowed on him in France.

One block west of the site of Moreau's print shop, on 2nd Street at Walnut, is City Tavern, which was mentioned as a gathering place by both Chastellux and Moreau, as well as by many of the American notables in Philadelphia at the time. Today's building is a reconstruction dating from the 1976 Bicentennial. The fine restaurant within provides a bill of fare reflecting Philadelphia tastes in the late 18th century; servers are in period dress.

Just beyond, at 3rd and Walnut Streets, is the Merchant's Exchange. Built in 1834 as a center of finance and commerce, it is of Pennsylvania marble and a fine example of the modified Greek Revival style. The form of the building, whose lantern tower completes its silhouette, is a masterly adaptation to its site.

Just north of the Merchant's Exchange and predating it, on the west side of 3rd Street, stands another landmark, the First Bank of the United States. Its façade seems to announce the coming popular Greek Corinthian style. The American eagle in the pediment is of mahogany, now painted. In all probability it was carved by the French sculptor Legrand, since he said in 1797 that he had done "the marble colonnade, sculpture, carving, etc. of the portico of the new building of the Bank of the United States." When the First Bank of the United States lost its charter, this building was acquired by Stephen Girard, the immigrant from Bordeaux, and became the home of Girard's Bank, which remained a major Philadelphia bank for the next two centuries. [For more on Stephen Girard and Girard College, see The French in

Philadelphia: Highlights, and Benjamin Franklin Parkway & the Art Museum Area.]

Back in the vicinity of Independence Hall, on 5th Street below Chestnut, stand two important buildings of the American Philosophical Society. This first learned society in America—proposed and created by Benjamin Franklin—was founded in 1743 "to bring into contact the minds and knowledge of scientists and philosophers of Europe and America." Directly behind Old City Hall is Philosophical Hall, erected from 1785 to 1789. It is open to the public when APS-sponsored exhibits are on display there. Across 5th Street is the Society's Library, a reconstruction of the 1789 building which was the original home of the Library Company of Philadelphia, America's first circulating library. Inside is a veritable treasure-house of Americana. In a niche above the 5th Street door is a replica of a statue of Franklin adorned in a toga; the original, by Lazzarini, now stands in the lobby of the Library Company of Philadelphia in its present home, at 1314 Locust Street.

Through the years, many French citizens have been resident or foreign members, as well as officers, of the American Philosophical Society. During the 18th century, in addition to those already mentioned, these French names appear: Condorcet, Buffon, comte Otto, du Simitiere and Talleyrand. In the 19th century, among those with French connections were these members: Jean-Jacques Audubon, Pierre Duponceau, Irénée du Pont, comte Survillier (Joseph Bonaparte), Lucien Bonaparte, King Louis-Philippe, François-André Michaux, Louis Pasteur, Joseph E. Renan, Alexis de Tocqueville, Eugène Viollet-le-Duc.

Of the 19th century members, Duponceau (1760-1844) was one of Philadelphia's most distinguished scholars and for sixteen years (1828-1844) the Society's president. He was born in Île de Ré, France. Military careers were traditional in his family, but after his father's death, young Duponceau first tried studying for a religious life, which he found was not to his liking. He then went to Paris where he met baron von Steuben, who induced him to accompany him to America as his secretary and aide-de-camp. Duponceau left the army after two years and entered the business world in an office on the east side of 6th Street at Chestnut (the building was shared with the offices of the new State Department of the United States). Here he began to study law and was admitted to practice. He soon occupied a prominent place at the Philadelphia bar and frequently appeared before the United States Supreme Court.

Duponceau became a fine linguistic scholar and comparative philologist. His treatise on the Chinese language brought him a distinguished reputation abroad and at home. He also made scholarly studies of the American Indian languages. In addition to serving as president of the APS, he was president of the Athenæum of Philadelphia and of the newly formed Société de Bienfaisance de Philadelphie [for more, see Washington Square]. Today his portrait hangs in Library Hall of the Philosophical Society.

Through the 20th century, additional members of the APS had French connections. They included Raymond Aron, Joseph Bédier, Alexis Carel, Paul Cret, Marie Curie, Jean-Baptiste Duroselle, Claude Lévi-Strauss, Jean Monnet, Raymond Poincaré and others. From the 1770s to the present, more than two hundred French intellectuals have been elected to membership in the American Philosophical Society. For more information, phone 215-440-3400 or go to www.amphilsoc.org.

Benjamin Franklin,
American Philosophical Society

SOCIETY HILL

Not every Philadelphian knows that Society Hill takes its name from the fact that it is a portion of the 1681 settlement of the Free Society of Traders. What Philadelphians do know is that today this quarter constitutes one of the most harmonious and beautiful residential neighborhoods in America. It is the area directly south of Independence Park, running roughly from Walnut to South Streets and from Front to 6th or 7th Streets. As Philadelphia grew through its first two-and-a-half centuries, with its commercial center gradually moving west from the Delaware River, Society Hill remained largely intact. While it gradually declined as a desirable residential neighborhood, much of its housing stock remained.

Starting in the 1950s, progressive urban planners with access to city government encouraged the renovation of this area. Eighteenth-century houses were restored and modern townhouses built in their midst. A handful of apartment towers followed where larger tracts were available. Today, Society Hill contains some of the most desirable—and expensive—housing in the Philadelphia area. Every leafy street and alleyway can be toured on foot (there is no real hill to master in Society Hill). This district is said to hold more eighteenth-century houses in the Georgian style than any city outside London.

An excellent example of such a house contains beautiful period furnishings and can be visited by the public. **The Powel House**, at 244 South 3rd Street, was built in 1765 as the home of Samuel Powel, the last mayor of Philadelphia under the British Crown and the first mayor under the new Federal government. The house was a social center in its day—Mrs. Powel was a brilliant hostess—and here were entertained Washington, Jefferson, Franklin, John Adams, Lafayette, French officers and other distinguished visitors to the city. The marquis de Chastellux, who was a frequent guest of the Powels, describes Samuel Powel as "a man of considerable fortune who has traveled in Europe and brought back from there a taste for the fine arts: his house is adorned with valuable prints and good copies of several Italian paintings."

Powel graduated in 1760 from the newly established College of Philadelphia (now the University of Pennsylvania, also founded by Benjamin Franklin). He embarked on a seven year "grand tour" of Europe and upon his return married Elizabeth Willing. He devoted much time to public service and was a charter member of the American Philosophical Society. He died in 1793, a victim of the yellow fever.

Of Mrs. Powel, Chastellux said, "she received me in a handsome house furnished in the English manner and what pleased me most it was adorned with fine prints—Mrs. Powel has read a good deal and profitably—what chiefly distinguishes her is her taste for conversation and the truly European manner in which she uses her art and knowledge." On another occasion, he added, "I shall mention my dinner this day at Mrs. Powel's only to say that it was excellent and agreeable in every respect." John Adams was more outspoken in a letter to Abigail after dining at the Powels'; he reported that "the number of courses and the desserts were sinful."

The Powel house is open to the public from Thursday through Saturday, 12 noon to 5 p.m., Sunday 1 to 5 p.m. The last tours are at 4 p.m.

Just south of the Powel House there stood from 1787 to 1847 the palatial Mansion House, residence of William Bingham (1752-1804) and his wife Anne (1764-1801), who was Elizabeth Powel's niece. The Binghams entertained lavishly, and their hospitality was legendary. Shortly after their marriage, they had traveled to England and France. On their return to Philadelphia, they occupied the mansion they had built.

Anne Bingham was both beautiful and observant. Thomas Jefferson once asked her if she did not "truly and honestly find the tranquil pleasures of America preferable to the empty bustle of Paris." She replied in a June 1787 letter that reveals her character and feminist spirit:

I agree with you that many of the fashionable pursuits of the Parisian ladies are rather frivolous, and become uninteresting to the reflective mind; but the picture you have exhibited is rather overcharged [. . .] . The state of society in different countries requires corresponding Manners and Qualifications; those of the French women are by no means calculated for [. . .] America [. . .] . But you must confess that they are more accomplished and understand the Intercourse of Society better than in any other country. We are irresistibly pleased with them, because they possess the happy Art of making us pleased with ourselves; [. . .] the women of France interfere in the politics of the Country, and often give a decided turn to the Fate of Empires. Either by the gentle Arts of persuasion, or by the commanding force of superior Attraction and Address, they have obtained that Rank and Consideration in Society which the sex are entitled to, and which they in vain contend for in other countries. We are, therefore, bound in Gratitude to admire and revere them [. . .] as much as the Friends of the Liberties of Mankind reverence the successful Struggles of the American Patriots.

During the French Revolution, when some of the French people who had entertained the Binghams arrived here as refugees, they were welcomed at the Mansion House. Among them were the vicomte de Noailles, comte de Volney, and the future King of the French, Louis-Philippe.

More than fifty years after Anne Bingham's death, the eighty-eight-year-old Samuel Breck wrote of her, "Mrs. Bingham stood above competition in her day; nor has anyone of equal refinement in address, or social stateliness and graceful superintendence of a splendid establishment been produced in any circle in our city."

After the deaths of Anne and William Bingham, their house became a fine hotel, then slowly declined. In 1847, it was destroyed by fire and the land was bought by Michael Bouvier, a French *émigré*. More than two centuries later, his great-great granddaughter, Jacqueline Bouvier Kennedy, would become first lady of the United States in 1961 [for more on Michael Bouvier, see The French in Philadelphia: Highlights].

On the Mansion House land, Michael Bouvier built a row of brownstone houses, still standing on 3rd Street, a few doors south of the Powel House. The family resided in the middle one before moving to a fine mansion on North Broad Street. Always a devout Catholic family, they were known for their charitable endeavors. Michael Bouvier was a director of the Société de Bienfaisance de Philadelphie, then became its president (1869-1874). One daughter became a nun and another, Emma Bouvier Drexel, the stepmother of an American saint. St. Katharine Drexel (1858-1955) was canonized by Pope John Paul II in 2000; she had fostered a movement that raised millions in contributions for schools for American Indians and African-Americans. Most members of the first generation of American Bouviers are buried in St. Mary's churchyard on South 4th Street. The next generation, having entered the world of finance, settled in New York.

Facing the Powel and Bouvier houses on the east side of 3rd Street is a row of townhouses designed by I. M. Pei in the 1960s.

Although modernist in style, their scale is similar to that of older houses in the neighborhood. That has remained generally true of twentieth- and twenty-first-century row-houses built in Society Hill, which helps account for the harmony and charm of the neighborhood. Behind the Pei houses, in the interior courtyard accessible through a driveway from Locust Street, is a bronze casting of a floating figure by Gaston Lachaise (1886-1935), who came to the United States as a young sculptor from France in 1906. Beyond the Lachaise monument rise the Pei-designed Society Hill Towers, which were among the first—but not the last—high-rise dwellings in this and neighboring sections of Philadelphia. Today's skyline contrasts remarkably with what Chateaubriand saw when he visited Philadelphia in 1791. He described it as "a beautiful city with wide streets, planted with trees," but "with a monotonously low sky line [containing] no tall buildings or monuments."

At 125-129 Spruce Street squats the diminutive Man Full of Trouble Tavern. Built in 1759, it is the last remaining colonial-era tavern still standing in Philadelphia. Now owned by the University of Pennsylvania, it is not open to the public. Two streets to the south on nearby 2nd Street lies New Market, also known as Head House Square, which extends from Pine to Lombard Streets. Built between 1745 and 1804, the square was typical of those where an eighteenth-century market would develop. An unexpected widening of the street permitted market sheds, or shambles, to be built down the middle of the street. This is the only remaining market square in Philadelphia. The restored Head House at the center once was used to store fire-fighters' equipment.

Many of the older houses in Society Hill still display their old fire-marks, which are typically seen high up on the front wall. They identified the company that insured the house and provided a system of quasi-volunteer fire fighters. The first of these companies was organized by (who else?) Benjamin Franklin in 1736.

One block west of Head House Square, at 3rd and Pine Streets, is **St. Peter's Church (1761)**, surrounded by a graveyard where a number of prominent early Philadelphians lie buried, among them, the mother-in-law of Moreau de Saint-Méry. The white interior of this Episcopal church is typical of the gracefully simple architecture of colonial America. Its pews are boxed in and its graceful wine-glass pulpit and reading desk stand at the opposite end from the chancel.

Little more than a block from St. Peter's, on the corner of 4th and Delancey Streets, stands the Physick House, dating from 1786. It is the only remaining example of a large free-standing Federal era residence in Philadelphia. In 1790, it became the home of Dr. Philip Syng Physick, who was the leading American surgeon of his day.

The **Physick House** contains some of the finest Empire furniture in the city, much of it replete with Napoleonic motifs. In the drawing room is a painting presented to Dr. Physick by Joseph Bonaparte; a fine Aubusson rug is in the study and up-

stairs, in the headquarters of the Society of the Cincinnati, are candlesticks that Lafayette presented to Washington. The Society of the Order of the Cincinnati was created after the War of Independence by the officers of Washington's army, which included the French army and naval officers. Membership has been handed down to the present day from the eldest son of these officers to the eldest sons of succeeding generations. There are thirteen chapters in the United States (one for each of the original colonies) and one in France.

The Physick House is open for guided tours Thursday through Saturday, 12 noon to 5 p.m. and Sunday, 1 to 5 p.m. The last tour departs at 4:00 p.m.

Dr. Physick was one of a group of courageous people who cared for victims of the terrible yellow fever epidemic in 1793. From 1794 to 1816, he was a member of the staff of Pennsylvania Hospital. [see Washington Square].

Around the corner from the Physick House, at 322 Spruce Street, once stood the house where Louis-Philippe, the future "citizen-king" of France, lived in 1796, the first year of his exile in Philadelphia. The twenty-three-year-old duc d'Orléans, as he then was known, stayed as the guest of the Reverend William Marshall and his family. Nearly thirty-five years later, Lafayette would proclaim Louis-Philippe "king of the French, by the grace of God and the will of the people."

At 427 Spruce is the **Williams-Mathurin House** (below). Built in 1791, it is the only eighteenth-century diplomatic legation known to be still standing in the city. Its first occupant was comte René-Charles Mathurin de la Forest, Consul General of France. A later resident was Don José de Jaudenes, a commissioner of King Charles IV of Spain. The restored house is now a private residence. Its next-door neighbor is a handsome house that in 1796 was the residence of James Madison and his wife, Dolley. Madison would serve as President of the United States from 1809-1817. Before they were married in 1794, Dolley had been the young widow of John Todd, who died in the yellow fever epidemic of 1793. The Todd house, on Walnut at 4th Street, is open to the public.

A few steps north of Spruce Street on Fourth stands **Old St. Mary's Church** (1763) which, in 1808, with the appointment of the first Roman Catholic bishop for the United States, became Philadelphia's first Catholic cathedral. The severe brick façade is crisply trimmed in white. Inside is a dramatic sculpture of the Pietà by Alfred Boucher, a nineteenth-century French artist and contemporary of Rodin.

In the graveyard are many French names; they include soldiers in the Revolution as well as Acadians who came here after they were expelled from their homeland in the 1750s. Among the French buried here are Michael Bouvier and members of his family, along with two other early French settlers whose descendants have contributed in various ways to the development of the nation. One is Stephen (Étienne) Tourison (1756-1848), who was born in Bordeaux, became a soldier of the French Army in America, and eventually resided in Philadelphia. His descendants became known in the construction business. The other, Jacques-Antoine Laussat, sieur de Tétignac, came to Philadelphia in 1798, became a citizen, married, and settled here. His daughter's marriage to Emile-Camille Geyelin established a prominent Philadelphia family.

On the southwest corner of 4th and Locust is the eighteenth-century Shippen House, now the Church House for the Episcopal Diocese of Pennsylvania. After 1798, it became the home of Caspar Wistar, a leading physician of his day. He wrote the first American textbook on anatomy and was president of the American Philosophical Society (the lavish imported vine, Wistaria, with its grape-like clusters of purple blossoms, was named in Wistar's honor). The house's French connection lay with its first owner, William Shippen, and in the romantic attachment of his daughter Nancy to comte Guillaume Otto, the French Legation's *chargé d'affaires* in the 1780s. Forced by her father to marry another man, Nancy's letters and journal reveal her love for Otto and her unhappiness in her marriage.

Old St. Joseph's Church (photo on page 8) lies tucked away in a courtyard off Willings Alley near 4th Street. Founded in 1733, it is the oldest Catholic Church in Philadelphia. At its founding, St. Joseph's was also the only place in the English-speaking world where public celebration of the Mass was permitted by law. Here the marquis de Lafayette, comte de Grasse, comte de Rochambeau, many French officers, and—on occasion—General Washington attended Mass.

St. Joseph's registers record the births, marriages and deaths of its parishioners, among them the French Acadians, some of whom may have ended their sad destiny in the Quaker Alms House which stood behind the church on Walnut Street between 3rd and 4th Streets. According to legend, it is in St. Joseph's that Evangeline and Gabriel of Longfellow's poem are buried, although Longfellow himself used Holy Trinity Church, at 6th and Spruce Streets, as the site of the burial.

In the Quaker enclave, probably at the southeast corner of 4th and Willings Alley, was located the African School. Founded by Anthony Benezet and built in 1793 by the Society of Friends, it launched a new educational policy: co-education. Though beset by the problem of obtaining adequate funds and qualified teachers, the school survived for some years. A French visitor, Brissot de Warville, was particularly impressed by "the effect of the instruction on the demeanor of female pupils."

Finally, Locust between 4th and 5th Streets provides a characteristic, parting glimpse of Society Hill and its link to the city's historic past. On the northwest corner of 4th Street, across from the Shippen House, a small flower garden leads west past several well-tended eighteenth-century houses, a magnolia garden on the south side of the block, and a rose garden, which extends to Walnut Street, on the north. Today the houses are the residences of Independence Park administrators. The gardens invite strollers to enter for a few moments' rest and reflection.

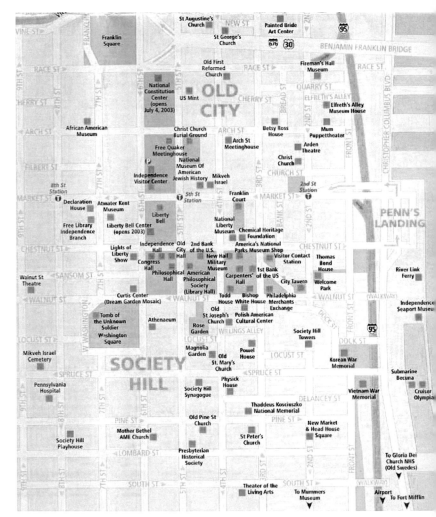

SOCIETY HILL & OLD CITY
(National Park Service, Department of the Interior)

OLD CITY

The area bounded roughly by Market and Vine, Front and 6ᵗʰ Streets was the northernmost portion of dense Philadelphia during the 18ᵗʰ and early 19ᵗʰ centuries. Then it turned into a factory and warehouse district throughout the long period when Philadelphia was a major manufacturing center. Today, this area is now generally referred to as Old City and is a fascinating mix of art galleries, loft apartments carved out of the earlier industrial buildings, specialty shops and theaters, all intermixed with remnants of Philadelphia's earliest years. Along the adjacent riverfront, which once was industrial, modern apartment towers are rising to the north and south of the Benjamin Franklin Bridge. At night, former piers now throb with discos, restaurants and clubs.

At the western edge of this district, between Race and Vine and 6ᵗʰ and 7ᵗʰ Streets, is Franklin Square (originally, Northeast Square), one of the original parks established by William Penn for Philadelphia. Today it is rather hemmed in by expressways and approaches to them, although it is undergoing a make-over at a time when nearby residential redevelopment is proceeding. The National Constitution Center is also just across from its southeast corner.

As Franklin Court reveals, Market Street in the 18ᵗʰ century was both a residential and a busy commercial thoroughfare. Here, as well as along Chestnut Street, several French dentists had their offices. These people were refugees from the revolutions in the West Indies and in France where, since the sixteenth century, the art of dentistry had been the most advanced in all of Europe. When they fled from their homelands, a number of them came to Philadelphia, which was then the most important city in the United States. The loss of these professionals, which was unfortunate for France, was most fortunate for the City of Brotherly Love. According to one account, at the start of the 19ᵗʰ century, "there was only one dentist in Philadelphia [. . .] tooth brushes were unknown; [. . .] one rubbed one's teeth with a rag on the end of a stick." Worse, it was said "that a man who washes his teeth was considered effeminate."

Announcements that appeared in Philadelphia papers told something of the immigrant dentists' techniques: They "transplant teeth, extract them, fit them on hooks, sell elixirs against scurvy." A Mr. Planton, recently arrived from France, had perfected what today is called a partial plate—putting teeth on hooks—as his 1818 advertisement graphically shows.

Incorruptible terro Metallic *TEETH*
Mr. Planton
Surgeon Dentist

Another announces: "Doctor le Mayeur, lately from New York, has taken lodgings at Mrs. Greenfield's, five doors above the Conestoga Wagon, in Market Street. Any persons disposed to sell their Front Teeth or any of them, may call on Dr. le Mayeur at his lodgings and receive two guineas for each tooth."

Dr. Lebreton's office was on Chestnut Street above 4th; M. Clambeau's, between Front and 2nd; Dr. Gardette (who had come with the troops as a regimental dentist) was established at 4th and Chestnut. In his ad, he gives the prices for "cleaning, curing the toothache, for each artificial tooth, for a toothbrush, etc." He also adds, compassionately, "teeth drawn for the poor gratis." Thanks to these and other French refugees, the profession of dentistry became well established here, with Philadelphia as the center for its development.

At Second just above Market Street stands Christ Church (built 1727-1744), Philadelphia's colonial church par excellence. Here worshipped many of the country's distinguished citizens, some of whose pews are marked with bronze plaques. They include Washington, Franklin, Betsy Ross, Adams, and Lafayette. This fine example of Georgian architecture contains the first palladian window in America, behind the altar, as well as the font in which William Penn was baptized. The tower and steeple were completed in 1754 largely through the efforts of the energetic Benjamin Franklin, who conducted three lotteries for the purpose. The steeple bells rang in unison with the Liberty Bell when the signing of the Declaration of Independence was first announced.

A small graveyard lies beside the church, though its larger burial ground is at 5ᵗʰ and Arch Streets, where Franklin and his wife, Deborah, are interred. Seven signers of the Declaration of Independence are also buried on Christ Church ground.

Chastellux came to a service here after having attended a Quaker meeting. In probable reaction to Quaker austerity, he provided this description of Christ Church: "A handsome pulpit, placed before a handsome organ; a handsome minister in that pulpit, reading, speaking with truly theatrical grace."

North of Christ Church and above Arch to the east of 2ⁿᵈ Street is the diminutive **Elfreth's Alley**. This street is unique in the United States, for all its houses have been private dwellings continuously resided in since they were built in the early 18ᵗʰ century. They are modest dwellings and were the homes of tradespeople and artisans, who generally established themselves north of Market Street. For a brief time, Talleyrand stayed at number 139. The Elfreth's Alley Museum House, at number 124-126, is open Monday through Saturday from 10 a.m. to 5 p.m., and on Sunday from 12 noon to 5 p.m. For more information, see www.elfrethsalley.org.

At the Fireman's Hall Museum at 147 N. 2ⁿᵈ Street, visitors may get a sense of the history of fire fighting in America. In this restored 1902 firehouse, early firefighting equipment is displayed. Included are a  1790s hand pumper and a 1907 Metropolitan Steamer. Hours are Tuesday through Saturday, 9 a.m. to 4:30 p.m. Phone: 215-923-1438.

At 239 Arch Street is the Betsy Ross House. The story of how she made the first American flag was passed down by her descendants before it reached the general public nearly a century later. Knowing that she ran an upholstery business from her home, George Washington and two other members of the Continental Congress are said to have visited her in 1776 with a sketch for a flag of the new republic. This house museum interprets that story and her life in the context of late eighteenth-century Philadelphia. Hours are 10 a.m. to 5 p.m. daily April through September, and Tuesday through Sunday from October through March. See www.betsyrosshouse.org, or phone 215-686-1252.

At the corner of 4th and Arch Streets is the brick **Arch Street Meeting House**, a splendid example of Quaker simplicity. The building dates from 1804 and is on land given to the Religious Society of Friends in 1693 by William Penn. The basic austerity of the sect, which Chastellux noted, is plainly visible here. Visitors may obtain a pamphlet in French which explains Quaker beliefs.

Little more than a block to the west, across 5th Street from the Christ Church burial ground, is the tiny Free Quaker Meeting House, which was founded in 1783 by Quakers who supported the War of Independence and so were "read out of meeting" by the pacifist members of the original meeting. Twice-widowed Betsy Ross was a member here, along with her third husband, John Claypoole. Because this building has not been home to an active group of Friends since 1834 (the aged Betsy Ross was one of the last two members who closed its doors permanently in that year), hours of opening are irregular; inquire at the Independence Visitor Center.

On the northeast corner of 5th and Arch Streets once stood (circa 1782) Pierre-Eugène du Simitiere's famous "American Museum" of natural and artificial curiosities. Du Simitiere (1735–1784) was described by Chastellux as a painter "from Geneva who had come to Philadelphia to make portraits and has remained there ever since; he is still a bachelor and a foreigner, a very uncommon thing in America." He was also an avid collector of books and pamphlets, many of which are in the

Promotional Broadside for du Simitiere's museum.
(Courtesy of the Library Company of Philadelphia.)

Library Company of Philadelphia collection. Through the efforts of French Minister Conrad Gérard, a number of du Simitiere's portraits of eminent Americans, made in Philadelphia about 1779, were engraved in Paris and thus preserved.

North on 4th Street, just below Vine Street, is St. Augustine's Church (Roman Catholic). Established in 1796 and dedicated in 1801, it was the first permanent establishment of the Augustinian Order in the United States and the largest church then in the city. It soon became the center of Catholic social life in Philadelphia. Michael Bouvier and Louise Vernon were married here in 1828. The old clock of Independence Hall and its original bell, preceding the Liberty Bell, once were housed in this church.

In the 1840s, when **St. Augustine's Church** had grown to have some three thousand parishioners, anti-Catholic (and anti-immigrant) sentiment grew in the city, fueled by political extremists who would become known as the Know-Nothing Party. On May 8, 1844, after three days of anti-Catholic rioting in Philadelphia, the church was burned to the ground and, with it, one of the largest theological libraries on the continent. The Augustinian  Order sued in Federal court and, in what was an early test of religious freedom under the First Amendment of the U.S. Constitution, rebuilt their church with the funds awarded. In 1847, the current church was completed. Its architect was the French Napoléon le Brun, who would also design Philadelphia's Academy of Music and the Roman Catholic Basilica of Saints Peter and Paul. [see Avenue of the Arts and Benjamin Franklin Parkway respectively].

Between 4th and 5th Streets above Market Street is the National Museum of American Jewish History (hours are 10 a.m. to 5 p.m., Monday through Thursday; 10 a.m. to 3 p.m. on Friday; and 12 noon to 5 p.m. on Sunday) and the adjoining Congregation Mikveh Israel. Founded in 1740, this is Philadelphia's oldest (Sephardic) Jewish congregation, although its place of worship is a modern building. It traces its beginnings to the petition made in 1740 by Nathan Levy to Thomas Penn, Pennsylvania's Royal Proprietor, for a plot of land in which he could bury his child in accordance with Jewish ritual. That grant became the basis of Mikveh Israel cemetery, between 8th and 9th on Spruce Street. The cemetery's most famous grave is that of Rebecca Gratz, the real-life model for Sir Walter Scott's heroine in Ivanhoe.

During the War of Independence, Jews from a number of American cities resettled in Philadelphia. A new synagogue was built on Cherry Street in 1782. In 1788, in the effort to pay the debt incurred by the building, members of the congregation addressed an appeal to "worthy fellow Citizens of every religious Denomination." Benjamin Franklin was among those who responded with a contribution, as did a number of other leading citizens. For more information, go to www.nmajh.org.

Finally, visitors to Old City should not fail to notice its lively art scene. If they venture here on the First Friday evening of every month, they will join multitudes who gather when the galleries throw open their doors, offering avant-garde exhibits along with wine and cheese. Experimental and repertory theater also thrives  in this quarter—at the Arden Theater, the Mum Puppettheater, and the Painted Bride Art Center. In September, Old City is the bustling heart of the Philadelphia Live Arts Festival and Philly Fringe, which brings hundreds of cutting-edge performing arts events to the city. For information, go to www.pafringe.com.

WASHINGTON SQUARE

The peaceful park between 6th and 7th Streets in the block south of Walnut Street, one of the four green spaces that Penn laid out in each quadrant of his new city, was simply Southeast Square until 1825, when all four were given their current names. Now under the jurisdiction of Independence National Park, Washington Square is the anchor of a mixed commercial and residential neighborhood that holds a special role in Philadelphia's past and an important place in its contemporary life. **(Washington Square map follows this section.)**

Originally, two roads and a little stream meandered across this six-acre park. In 1706, it was designated by Philadelphia's City Council "for a common and public burying ground." During the Revolutionary War, many prisoners who died of wounds or illness, both British and American, were buried there. They were joined by a number of African-Americans, displaced Acadians, paupers, and victims of the yellow fever.

Early in the 19th century, the square is said to have been a frequent site for African-American festivities. According to one contemporary account, as many as a thousand black Philadelphians came to what they reportedly called Congo Square "to dance after the manner of their several nations in Africa, speaking and singing in their native dialects." They could be seen "going to the graves of their friends early in the morning, and there leaving them gifts of victuals and rum."

Although Washington Square ceased to serve as a burial ground after the 1793 yellow fever epidemic, it became the fitting site, in the mid-twentieth century, of the **Tomb of the Unknown Soldier**

of the American Revolution. Standing over the sarcophagus, just west of the central pool and fountain, is a majestic bronze statue of Washington. This is a recasting of the only full-length statue of the nation's first president that was done from life; the original stands in the rotunda of the capitol of Virginia in Richmond. It was made by the French artist Jean-Antoine Houdon (1741-1828), the greatest portrait sculptor of his time.

Thanks to Houdon, we have accurate likenesses of a number of America's early heroes: John Paul Jones (a replica is in the Pennsylvania Academy of Fine Arts), Thomas Jefferson, Benjamin Franklin, George Washington, Robert Fulton, Joel Barlow. All but Washington sat for him while they were in France. Houdon was also part scientist. He made moldings of shoulders and facial bones and measured his subjects with scientific instruments so that his portrait busts are both life-size and accurate to the millimeter. When the Virginia General Assembly voted to commission a statue of Washington, Thomas Jefferson, the new U.S. Minister to France, remarked "there could be no question about the sculptor who should be employed; the reputation of Monsieur Houdon . . . being unrivaled in Europe." Franklin, then ready to leave Paris, invited the sculptor to come to America. He did so, went to Mt. Vernon, and there Washington sat for him.

In 1815, Washington Square was declared a park. Some eighteen years later, it was laid out with geometric paths and hundreds of trees were planted. By 1846, the one-time burial ground had become a "beautiful and fashionable promenade." In 1853, the American landscape architect, Andrew Jackson Dowling, could write in *Rural Essays* that Washington Square contained "more well grown specimens of forest trees than any similar space of ground in America." When, in 1915, a count was made of the original plantings extant, around 104 varieties still stood, some rare to the region. Today, great shade trees still dominate the park.

A noted French botanist, François-André Michaux (1746-1802) had been engaged to select the trees originally. He came to America in 1785 on a French government scientific mission proposed by the then French Consul in New York, St. Jean de Crèvecœur. The mission resulted in the establishment of nurseries in New Jersey and in Charleston, South Carolina, for the cultivation of American plants to be shipped to France. Michaud's records of his extensive travels here and his descriptions of the plant life he found played an essential role in the study and classification of the flora of North America.

His son, François Michaux (1770–1855), continued his father's work. While in Philadelphia, he replanted the trees in Washington Square. Having met and admired Dr. Caspar Wistar [see Society Hill] he gave the name Wistaria to a vine imported from the Orient. In 1809 he was elected to membership in the American Philosophical Society, and his portrait hangs in Library Hall.

Opposite Washington Square's southeast corner, on 6th Street, stands the former headquarters—now an art gallery—in the Beaux-Arts style, of the Lea and Febiger Publishing Company, founded by Mathew Carey. Carey (1760–1839) was a fiery young Irish pamphleteer in whom Benjamin Franklin became interested while in Paris, recommending him to Lafayette. Carey eventually came to Philadelphia and with $400 lent him by Lafayette established a printing business and a bookstore, and soon enjoyed a respected position in business.

Washington Square became the publishing headquarters of Philadelphia in the 19th century. In addition to Lea and Febiger, J. B. Lippincott & Co. publishers were based in a red brick building facing the square on 6th Street (the building is now a luxury condominium); on the square's southeast corner, at 7th Street, was the home of the Farm Journal (now a Pennsylvania Hospital building); the W. B. Saunders Company (also a condominium today) was at the corner of 7th and Locust Streets.

On Walnut, facing the square, is the block-long Curtis Center, built to house the Curtis Publishing Company. Its most famous and popular magazine, the *Saturday Evening Post*, was America's oldest, dating from 1728. It had some six million subscribers by 1960, shortly before Curtis ceased publication of this and several other magazines. Today, the Curtis Center has been transformed into a modern office complex. What once was an open delivery court is now a soaring neo-Egyptian atrium (enter on 7th Street). The 6th Street lobby is home to the spectacular "Dream Garden" mosaic, designed by Maxfield Parrish and executed in more than 100,000 pieces of favrile glass by the studios of Louis Comfort Tiffany. It was commissioned by

Cyrus Curtis and installed here in 1916. Both the lobby and courtyard are open during business hours.

On January 9, 1793, the Washington Square area must have bubbled with excitement. At 6ᵗʰ and Walnut Streets, where the Penn Mutual Insurance Company building now stands, an unprecedented vision arose from the courtyard of what then was the site of the Walnut Street Prison. Pierre Blanchard (1750–1809) ascended far above the prison walls in a hot-air balloon. Blanchard had repeatedly dazzled Paris with this new invention, and in 1785 had crossed the English Channel in a balloon with an American, Dr. John Jeffries of Boston. This was the first time such an event had taken place in America.

The ascension in the then-capital city was witnessed by a group of distinguished Philadelphians: President and Mrs. Washington; James Madison; Jean de Ternant, the French minister; Pierre-Charles L'Enfant, who was drawing plans for the future capital city of Washington; Dr. Caspar Wistar; Dr. Benjamin Rush; Benjamin Franklin Bache; Peter Legaux; David Rittenhouse; Pierre Duponceau; Charles Willson Peale; Stephen Girard; and members of the diplomatic corps. The streets were filled with people, who craned from windows and rooftops.

A cannon was fired, and with a flourish of his plumed hat, Blanchard allowed his balloon to rise. It reached an altitude of more than a mile and crossed the Delaware River before being brought down at what is now Deptford, near Woodbury, New Jersey. The consternation—and fright—of the natives might have had dire consequences, for Blanchard knew no English and couldn't explain that he wasn't a man from Mars. Fortunately, President Washington had given him a *passe-port* letter of introduction which explained things to everyone's satisfaction. Blanchard opened a bottle of wine—which he had thoughtfully brought with him—and everyone was happy. The balloon was carefully folded, a team was brought to get it out of the woods, and Blanchard returned to Philadelphia in triumph the same evening.

In January 1976, on the 183ʳᵈ anniversary of Pierre Blanchard's feat, a renowned twentieth-century balloonist, Constance Wolf, re-enacted the ascension. The lift-off on this occasion was from Independence Mall, north of Market Street.

Also in 1793, a terrible yellow fever epidemic struck Philadelphia. Several thousands died, from every walk of life. Mayor Samuel Powel was one of the victims, as was John Todd, Dolley Todd Madison's first husband. Those who could do so fled the city; those who stayed to care for the sick were heroes. The cause of yellow fever was still unknown. Philadelphia doctors generally followed the treatment favored by the highly respected Dr. Rush, who energetically bled the sick, which weakened them, so that many died.

In the midst of the plague, city officials received a committee's report on the deplorable condition of Bush Hill, the city hospital. To their surprise, two members of that committee, French-born businessman Stephen Girard, and Peter Helm, a cooper and devout Moravian, offered their services to establish greater order in the hospital. Once their offer was accepted, they divided the work—Helm to oversee the external needs (buildings, supplies, etc.) and Girard to care for the rooms, the sick, and the general administration. Girard reorganized the hospital. He was ably assisted both by Helm and by Dr. Jean Devèze, a refugee from Saint-Domingue, a "first-class health officer of the French armies at Cap François." Girard, with his usual acumen, had spotted him as a possible valuable aide who, like himself, did not believe the fever to be contagious. Devèze was urged to offer his services. After much dickering with the Rushites, who were loath to admit the alternative medical procedures of an alien culture, Girard was granted his demand. The team of Girard, Helm, and Devèze—with the clerical help of Dr. Benjamin Duffield—succeeded in saving countless lives.

During that same dreadful year of 1793, the French Benevolent Society of Philadelphia (La Société de Bienfaisance de Philadelphie) was founded to bring aid to persons of French extraction who "have been or shall become reduced to want by misfortune and not by bad conduct." The origins of the Society date to two years earlier when, because of the French Revolution, large numbers of French people felt obliged to flee the country. Many came to America and settled in Philadelphia. No sooner had the refugees arrived than they began to organize among themselves. Later, the revolution in Saint-Domingue caused hundreds of the French to flee the island; ship after ship arrived in Philadelphia filled with gaunt, hungry, sickly passengers who told of the British privateers who had boarded the ships and seized the refugees' property. It was a sad lot of refugees that kept arriving during the hot August days of 1793. In the face of such tragedy, the Society was established. Its first president was the French Minister Plenipotentiary, chevalier Jean-Baptiste de Ternant (1751-1816).

According to Chastellux, who first met him at a dinner given by the Minister de la Luzerne, Ternant was "a French officer in the service of America—a young man of great wit and talent; he draws well and speaks English like his own language; he was made a prisoner at Charlestown." He was esteemed by Washington, who found in him "a man who seems to belong to both countries." Ternant returned to America in 1791 as the last representative of the French monarchy; when the monarchy fell, in 1793, he chose to remain in America. He was succeeded as France's Minister Plenipotentiary by Citizen Genet.

The Society remained an active force in Philadelphia for two centuries. Through the years, many prominent individuals acted as its officers, including la Forêt, Duponceau, Benjamin Armand, the prince de Joinville, Napoléon III, Michael Bouvier and Joseph Bonaparte.

A grand house-that-never-was might have been completed one block above Washington Square had one man's fortunes lasted. In the 1790s, the famous French architect Pierre-Charles L'Enfant designed a grand marble and brick mansion for Robert Morris (1734-1806), then one of the nation's leading business-men, a former United States senator and the financier of the American Revolution. Its property would have filled the block bounded by Chestnut, Walnut, 7th and 8th Streets. While con-struction was underway, Morris went bankrupt as the result of his speculation in western land; for three years, he was impris-oned as a debtor. The unfinished house was unsalable and finally was demolished in about 1800. L'Enfant went on to be remembered for his city plan of the new national capital in Washington, DC.

On the east side of Washington Square, on 6th Street, is the handsome Athenæum of Philadelphia. It is one of a handful of such institutions left in America—a private library in which the members own shares which can be, and are, handed down from generation to generation. In 1814, a group of Philadelphia's leading citizens established the Athenæum as a "convenient place of common resort in which leisure hours could be passed." The charter of 1815 states: "This association is for the purpose of procuring newspapers of different states and countries, pamphlets, books, maps, charts and collecting historical and other monuments connected with the history and antiquities of America, and the useful arts, and generally to disseminate useful knowledge."

The **Athenæum** originally was located above Mathew Carey's bookstore at 4th and Chestnut Streets but moved into its present building in 1847. One of the first American buildings clad in native brownstone, it was designed by the American architect, John Notman, and is one of the seminal buildings in the country in the Italianate Revival style. The Athenæum's remarkable collection, invaluable for scholarly  research in many fields, is especially rich in American architectural history.

The Athenæum displays a fascinating collection of paintings, sculpture, and decorative pieces associated with the long American residence of Joseph Bonaparte, who created an estate—Point Breeze—at nearby Bordentown, New Jersey, where he spent most of his time from 1817 to 1832. A twentieth-century descendant of Bonaparte's friend and physician, Dr. Edmund L. DuBarry (1797–1853), made most of this collection available to the Athenæum. Included are pieces from the former king's personal art collection, as well as porcelain, portraits, and furniture he owned, some of which was made by Michael Bouvier.

The building's second floor contains the elegant reading room, which today looks almost exactly as it did when the building first opened in the mid-nineteenth century. The roster of officers and members of the Athenæum includes a long list of distinguished, civic-minded Philadelphians, among them Pierre Duponceau, who was the institution's second president. The Athenæum may be visited by appointment. For hours, go to www.philaathenaeum.org.

Just south of Washington Square, at 6th and Spruce Streets, is the **Holy Trinity Catholic Church**, built in 1789. Although founded for German Catholics, it very soon became the parish church for refugees from Acadia, France, and Saint-Domingue, as the names on the tombstones indicate. Stephen Girard was first buried here, before his remains were removed to Founder's Hall of Girard College.

This quaint church is associated with the legend of Evangeline, made famous by Longfellow's epic poem of the same name. Longfellow evidently spoke of Holy Trinity when he said, "I placed the final scene, the meeting between Evangeline and Gabriel and the death, at the poor house, and the burial in an old Catholic graveyard not far away." The actual models for Longfellow are believed to be buried at St. Joseph's Church [see Society Hill].

Just to the west of the church and across Spruce Street is number 626, which was the site of Madame Buchey's French and English Boarding and Day School for Young Ladies from 1830 to 1853. This excerpt from an announcement in the National Gazette gives an interesting glimpse of a girls' school curriculum early in the 19th century:

August 24, 1833
MRS. BUCHEY'S FRENCH AND ENGLISH
Boarding and Day School for Young Ladies,
Spruce Street below Seventh

The course of Instruction in this Institution includes the following branches: viz. Reading, Writing, Arithmetic, Grammar, Geography with the use of the Globes, History, Rhetoric and Composition, Natural Philosophy, Chemistry, Needle-work, Rug-work, and Fancy Painting, in various styles; Music, Singing and Playing on the Piano, and the Guitar.

In the management of the School, mildness is united with as much strictness as it is deemed indispensable for inspiring the youthful mind with a due regard for propriety, and a clear determination of right and wrong. The Instruction is adapted to the capacity of the learner, and conveyed in the manner best calculated to develop the powers of the understanding, storing it with special knowledge, while the greatest attention is paid to the formation of the moral character and gentle deportment.

The pupils learning French will have the best opportunity for speaking it with fluency and correctness, and as infancy is the proper time for acquiring the true sound of a foreign language, they will be received either as Boarders or Day Scholars, at the earliest age possible.

References: Rev. Bishop Onderdonk, Rev. Bishop Keurick, rev. Mr. Hughes, Rev. Mr. W. E. Ashton.

The duties of the school will be resumed on the first of September.

Madame Buchey was a prominent French refugee who stayed in Philadelphia and whose descendants have continued the Francophile tradition. Born in 1800 in Port-au-Prince, she was the daughter of a French merchant who came to Philadelphia in 1803 as a refugee from the revolution there. In 1815, she was married at St. Joseph's Church to M. Buchey, a silk merchant from Angoulême, France. Several children were born to the couple. After her husband became an invalid, Madame Buchey established her school, which she ran successfully until 1853. It attracted young ladies from as far away as Cuba and Venezuela, in addition to those living nearby. A great-great grandson of Madame Buchey, Francis James Dallett, was a twentieth-century leader in the French Benevolent Society and for many years an archivist at the University of Pennsylvania.

At 8th and Spruce Streets is the busy, modern entrance to Pennsylvania Hospital—the first hospital in America, founded by Benjamin Franklin and Dr. Thomas Bond in 1751 "for the relief of the sick and the miserable." Today's east wing, between Spruce and Pine along 8th Street, was the original building; its cornerstone, with text by Franklin, is visible near the southeast corner. Moreau de Saint-Méry provided an early statistical report on the work of the hospital: "Up to March 1795, 9,000 patients had been admitted; almost 4,000 cured; 120 declared incurable." He added that there were "from 30 to 40 lunatics, most of them as a result of love."

Visitors should apply at the hospital's welcome desk (enter through the 8th Street entrance) for a walking tour of historic rooms. Hours are 8:30 a.m. to 4:30 p.m. Monday through Friday. Highlights include the 1804 surgical amphitheater at the top of the building where Dr. Philip Physick practiced [see Society Hill] and Benjamin West's 1815 painting, "Christ Healing the Sick in the Temple." Pennsylvania Hospital also houses an impressive historic collection in its medical library, the first in the nation. Its gardens along Pine Street are open to visitors. More information is at www.pennhealth.com/pahosp.

Clinton Street (below) is a quiet residential street, only two blocks long, running east and west between 9th and 11th Streets. For many years, at number 920, lived Agnès Repplier (1855–1950), a well-known essayist and biographer. Her book, *Père Marquette*, is an account of the remarkable French Jesuit missionary and explorer who, in 1673, accompanied Joliet as the first European explorers of the Mississippi River. Another biography, *Mère Marie of the Ursulines*, tells the story of the intrepid French nun who came to New France in Quebec's early days. *Philadelphia: The Place and the People*, gives a lively account of life in colonial Philadelphia and recreates the atmosphere of the city as the 20th century began.

At 253 South 10th Street, the first edition of *L'Indicateur Français de Philadelphie* was published in 1881. This directory of names and addresses of French-speaking residents was evidence of a local Francophile community active in the late 19th century in Philadelphia.

Just south of Locust at 260 South 9th Street is the **Joseph Bonaparte House**. After abdicating as king of Spain, Napoléon's brother resided here in 1815 and 1816 while his mansion was being built in Bordentown, New Jersey. Bonaparte's arrival in Philadelphia caused a considerable social stir. Members of the diplomatic corps and intellectuals from the scientific and literary world came to this house, as did the social elite. The house was beautifully decorated and furnished. In 1823, Bonaparte was elected a member of the American Philosophical Society, as was his brother, Lucien. Some of the contents are among the items on view at the Athenæum; others are now on display at Winterthur Museum near Wilmington, Delaware [see Country Mansions & Gardens]. The house is now a private residence, part of what is today called Bonaparte Court.

On the corner of 9th and Walnut Streets is the restored Regency-fronted Walnut Street Theatre, the oldest theater in the United States. It also claims to be the longest continuously-functioning theater in the English-speaking world. It opened in 1809 and, throughout the 19th century, presented all the finest American actors and most of the popular plays of the period. Today, it is home to a highly successful subscription company. For season programs and tickets, go to www.wstonline.org.

Wrapping around the corner of 10th and Chestnut Streets is a recently restored and revitalized building in the French Renaissance or Second Empire style. Like a number of other Center City buildings that have outlived their original purpose, the **Victory Building** has been turned into a residential condominium. Its resemblance to Philadelphia's City Hall reflects the architectural taste of the  1870s, when both buildings were constructed. They are among the most important such examples left in the United States today. Across the street is the former Federal Reserve Bank building designed in the Art Deco style in the 1930s by the Franco-American architect Paul-Philippe Cret [see Benjamin Franklin Parkway and Rittenhouse Square].

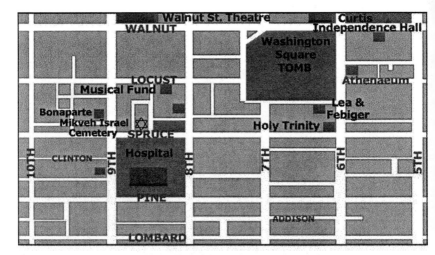

WASHINGTON SQUARE
Courtesy of ushistory.org (modified)

THE AVENUE OF THE ARTS DISTRICT

Philadelphia's north-south spine is Broad Street, which runs from the former Naval Base at the junction of the Schuylkill and Delaware Rivers in the south to the northern city boundary at Cheltenham Avenue, a distance of some sixteen miles. The mile or so of Broad Street that passes through Center City was rechristened the **Avenue of the Arts (map on final page of this section)** during the 1990s to draw attention to the many cultural institutions along this strip, especially below City Hall. Here and there, as elsewhere in the city, the French influence is evident.

The anchor of this street—as it is for all of downtown Philadelphia—is the massive **City Hall**, built where Broad (14ᵗʰ)' and Market Streets cross. The site was William Penn's Center Square, the only one of the five open spaces he planned for the city that has ceased to be a public park. Penn's vision for a city that stretched from river to river was not realized until the 19ᵗʰ century. In 1694, a Quaker meeting house had been built on Center Square, but it soon had to be abandoned as too far west. Through its next hundred years, Philadelphia's center remained well to the east of Broad Street. When Rochambau's soldiers marched "up" Chestnut Street in 1781, they were on their way to camps in Center Square. Soon after, it became the site of the city's water works and a green spot for fêtes, patriotic gatherings, and social promenades.

Meanwhile, Philadelphia's population was burgeoning. The city had at least 81,000 residents in 1800 and more than 408,000 in 1850; by 1900, there would be nearly 1,300,000. Such enormous growth north, west, and south sprawled well beyond the boundaries of Penn's original plan, but it finally put Center Square pretty squarely in the center of the city's commercial heart. That development was acknowledged in 1870, after some thirty-three years of debate, when Center Square was chosen in a public referendum as the site for a new Public Building, as the imagined new City Hall was then called.

Architects John McArthur, Jr. and Thomas Ustick Walter, chosen to plan the new building, designed it in the French Renaissance Style, modeling it loosely on the Louvre in Paris. It took a remarkable thirty years—1871 to 1901—to complete. Criticism began almost immediately, as did contractor-corruption trials. The slow pace of building accentuated the fact that its design was out of style long before this "marble elephant," as some derisively called the project, was completed. For decades afterward, a number of critics and city officials considered tearing it down. The last such serious proposal, in 1952, would have left only the tower as a traffic island.

Tastes in architecture come and go. By the 1960s, Center City was reviving, along with interest in Victorian architecture. City Hall began to be regarded in the way most see it today, as one of the most significant and beautiful nineteenth-century buildings in America. Now undergoing a multi-year cleaning, its pale granite walls, creamy marble columns, and ornate sculpture are nearly restored to their original luster. At night, its walls are bathed in ethereal light. It has always been stupendous. Filling most of its 4.5-acre site, it contains 750 rooms and 14.5 acres of floor space. It is covered with some 250 pieces of sculpture, all from the studio of Alexander Milne Calder. The carvings represent a complex iconography illustrating the founding, settling and development of Philadelphia and the region. At the pinnacle of the clock tower, 548 feet above street level, a 37-foot figure of William Penn gazes over his city. Near the west entrance to the courtyard, a bronze wall plaque notes that Rochambeau's troops camped on this spot on their way to Virginia and Yorktown.

Visits to the tower leave from room 121, inside the East Portal, every fifteen minutes, Monday through Friday, from 9:30 a.m. to 4:30 p.m. Views from the top are awesome. To see the building's elaborate interior—including the Mayor's Reception Room and ornate Conversation Hall (where Joseph Alexis Bailly's original marble likeness of George Washington stands)—and to learn more of its history, guided tours are essential. They are offered at 12:30 p.m. each weekday. Phone 215-686-2840 for more information.

Just north of City Hall, on the east side of Broad Street, is the Masonic Temple, the Grand Lodge of Pennsylvania for the Masonic Order. Built in 1873, the exterior is in the Norman-Romanesque style. Inside are seven grandly ornate lodge rooms representing a late-Victorian view of the principal architectural achievements of various historical epochs. Included are the decidedly French Norman and Renaissance Halls, as well as Corinthian, Egyptian, Gothic, Ionic, and Oriental Halls—all of which may be viewed on a guided tour of the building. For more information, go to www.pagrandlodge.org.

Two blocks north, at Broad and Cherry Streets, is the **Pennsylvania Academy of the Fine Arts.** The Academy was founded in 1805 by a group of art-minded citizens led by Charles Willson Peale—he of the many portraits [see Independence Park]. It is the oldest art museum and teaching academy in

America. One of the founding members was William Rush, the first American-born sculptor and wood-carver.

Any number of Academy students have become world famous artists, including many who studied and worked in Paris; among them are Philadelphians Mary Cassatt, Cecilia Beaux, Henry O. Tanner, and Thomas Eakins, who studied with Bonnat and Gérôme.

As a museum, the Academy has a fine collection of paintings and sculptures. Among the latter are several pieces by the noted French sculptor, Joseph Alexis Bailly (1822-1883). Bailly was the most noted sculptor in 1870s Philadelphia and one of the most respected in America. He was born in Paris, the son of a cabinet-maker. His talent was formed in the *ateliers* of Paris, but his studies were interrupted when, during the uprising of 1848, he seems to have been involved in an altercation and had to flee. He went first to New Orleans, then worked in Buenos Aires before coming to Philadelphia. Here he married, established his studio, and taught a generation of future artists at the Pennsylvania Academy.

At the Centennial Exposition of 1876, Bailly was well-represented by an equestrian portrait of Venezuela's President Guzman; a marble "Aurora" in the American gallery; and a figure of John Witherspoon, commissioned by the Presbyterian Women of America and mounted on Scottish granite. Besides the marble statue of George Washington in City Hall and its bronze recast in front of Independence Hall, there are two beautiful marbles of his in the Academy of the Fine Arts: "The Expulsion" and "The First Prayer."

The Academy has occupied its landmark building on the southwest corner of Broad and Cherry Streets since 1876. Designed by Philadelphia's pre-eminent architect of the period, Frank Furness, its galleries make a vibrant, colorfully Victorian showcase for displaying the Academy's holdings and changing exhibitions. On the Broad Street façade of the building are six small relief panels; these are a simplified copy of a hemicycle in the main lecture room of the École des Beaux-Arts in Paris, which thus proclaim a link with the French academic tradition. In 2005, the Academy opened its large new Samuel M. V. Hamilton Building, directly across Cherry Street. This stunning makeover of an industrial building provides vastly greater space for the school, studios and exhibitions. The Academy's exhibition hours are from 10 a.m. to 5 p.m. Tuesday through Saturday and from 11 a.m. on Sunday. Closed Mondays and holidays. For further information, go to www.pafa.org.

Only a few steps to the west of the Avenue of the Arts on Chestnut Street is a recent addition to Philadelphia's cultural life, the Prince Music Theater. This conversion of a movie theater has become America's home for new musical theater development. Its main stage presents a series of new and revived musicals annually. The Prince also provides a season of cabaret performances, new and classic films, and in summer, a studio progam to train young people in the craft of musical theater. Visit the website at www.princemusictheater.org.

Back on the Avenue of the Arts, two imposing nineteenth-century buildings rise at Sansom and, one block south, at Walnut Streets. The Union League has been, since the 1870s, the city's pre-eminent social club. From its construction in 1902–1904, the Bellevue-Stratford Hotel was its leading hotel. Since the 1980s, a smaller version of that hotel, the **Park Hyatt Philadelphia at the Bellevue**, has occupied the top floors while the lower floors contain high-end shops and restaurants. The hotel's Beaux-Arts style is lavishly displayed in the restaurant and lounges under the arched ceilings on the top floor.

At the southwest corner of Broad and Locust Streets is the Academy of Music, affectionately known as the Old Lady of Locust Street. It was built as the city's opera house in 1857 from the designs of French architect Napoléon Le Brun—who had studied the great opera houses of Europe—and Gustave Runge. The original plans called for a marble exterior to match the beautiful interior, but Philadelphia's conservatism suddenly reared its stubborn head. Sufficient funds were not made available and the "temporary" red-brick shell became permanent—contributing, incidentally, to the characteristic red-brick face of much of old Philadelphia.

The ordinary exterior belies the interior, which makes the Academy what many regard as the loveliest opera house in America. Resplendent in gold and marble, its auditorium is crowned with an ornately frescoed ceiling and brilliant chandelier, while the lobby, hallways, and ballroom all dazzle with faux-painted finishes. For more than a century after the founding of the Philadelphia Orchestra in 1900, the Academy was the Orchestra's home. Since the Orchestra's move to the Kimmel Center in December, 2001, the Academy is once again used primarily as an opera house. The Opera Company of Philadelphia and the Pennsylvania Ballet are both resident here, and many visiting companies in the performing arts are also presented on the Academy stage.

In the blocks south of the **Academy of Music** on the Avenue of the Arts are several more theaters, an art school, and the Kimmel Center for the Performing Arts. Designed by the noted architect Rafael Viñoly and completed in 2001, the Kimmel Center contains two major auditoriums for musical performances, as well as a small "black box" theater for smaller reviews and solo performers. Its exterior pays tribute to the red brick of the Academy of Music. Inside its vast, glass-domed plaza is a welcoming public space.

The new home of the Philadelphia Orchestra is the Kimmel's wood-burnished Verizon Hall, the interior of which curves in the sinuous shape of a cello. Other major symphony orchestras from around the world also play here when they visit Philadelphia. Peter Nero and the Philly Pops are also resident at Verizon. Near the front of the plaza, the smaller—and highly flexible—Perelman Theater is the residence of the modern dance troupe, Philadanco, the Chamber Orchestra of Philadelphia, the Philadelphia Chamber Music Society, and American Theater Arts for Youth. It is also the site for performances by visiting ensembles and soloists. The public spaces of the plaza and balconies provide a restaurant and bar; atop the Perelman, a terrace garden affords a close-up view of the barrel-vaulted glass ceiling. For more information, go to www.kimmelcenter.org.

Between the Academy of Music and the Kimmel Center stands the Merriam Theater, which presents a season of theatrical and musical performances brought to town by touring companies. Across the street, on the northeast corner of Spruce Street, is the Wilma Theater, which provides a lively series of plays, both new and in revival, to a subscription audience. On the corner of Broad and Pine Streets, across from the Greek Revival University of the Arts building, the Theater Company of Philadelphia will have its new home on the ground floor of Symphony Hall, a high-rise condominium. Further south is the Arts Bank Theater, on the southwest corner of Broad and South Streets. That converted bank building is the site for a variety of musical performances and experimental theater.

Two additional cultural institutions of note lie just off the Avenue of the Arts. The Historical Society of Pennsylvania is at the southwest corner of 13th and Locust Streets. Founded in 1824, its second president was Pierre Duponceau. The Society possesses a magnificent reference library, containing nearly 600,000 books, pamphlets, and microfilm reels; twenty million manuscripts, and more than 300,000 graphic items. They document the settlement and subsequent history of the Commonwealth. In 2002, the HSP acquired the holdings of the Balch Institute for Ethnic Studies, which added immeasurably to its sources for the study of ethnic communities and immigrant experiences of those more recently arrived in America. For more information on the HSP, go to www.hsp.org.

Courtesy of Avenue of the Arts, Inc. (modified) www.avenueofthearts.org

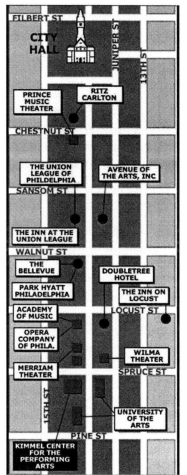

Next door to the Historical Society, at 1314 and 1320 Locust Street, is the current home of the Library Company of Philadelphia, one of the numerous brainchildren of Benjamin Franklin. As America's oldest cultural institution, founded in 1731, its research library collection documents every aspect of American history and culture from the colonial period through the end of the 19th century, housing half a million rare books, 75,000 vintage graphics, and 160,000 manuscripts. Peering out from a window over-looking the street is Francesco Lazzarini's massive statue of a toga-clad Benjamin Franklin, weather-worn from its years at the Library Company's original site on 5th Street. Other Franklin mementos abound. Over the card catalogue in the reading room is the earliest known painting of Philadelphia, a 1720 panorama by Peter Cooper, which was found rolled up in a London curiosity shop. Amidst an array of busts of early notables is one of Lafayette by Luigi Persico. In the adjacent Logan Room is a mirror from the famed Meschianza Ball held during the British occupation of Philadelphia. For more information on this first lending library in America, see www.librarycompany.org.

BENJAMIN FRANKLIN PARKWAY &
THE ART MUSEUM AREA

The Benjamin Franklin Parkway, Philadelphia's Avenue des Champs-Elysées, was designed early in the 20th century by the well-known French landscape architect, Jacques Gréber (1882-1962). His plan, which was based on proposals from the French architect Paul-Philippe Cret and prominent Philadelphia architects, called for a grand boulevard from City Hall to the new art museum to be built on the hill William Penn had called Faire Mount. Like its Paris model, the Parkway was conceived as part of a grand plan in urban renewal, cutting diagonally across Penn's grid of streets in a deteriorating neighborhood to create a new feeling of space and perspective. It would also provide a dramatic entry into Fairmount Park, leading to the banks of the Schuylkill River and beyond.

By the time the Parkway's plans were drawn up, the popularity of the French Second Empire style had run its course, so the architects turned to the French classic style then in favor. The boulevard itself was largely completed in 1917, at the time of the U.S. entry into World War I. The planners had intended that headquarters buildings of organizations dedicated to scientific, literary, civic, or artistic pursuits would flank both sides of the Parkway. Yet, because of two world wars linked by a crushing depression, most of that vision failed to materialize, at least not initially. Today, more than eighty years later, plans are underway for bringing two additional arts institutions to the Parkway. Once that is accomplished, and the Philadelphia Museum of Art completes its very ambitious plans for expansion, the Benjamin Franklin Parkway will be closer to realizing the planners' original dream for it than ever before.

Paul-Philippe Cret (1876-1945), French-born and French-educated, became a Philadelphian who bestowed an imposing number of buildings, monuments and bridges on this region, in addition to his design for the Parkway. His work in other cities included the Pan-American Union and the Folger Shakespeare Library in Washington, DC; Gettysburg's Eternal Light Memorial; and important buildings in Annapolis, West Point, Indianapolis, and Austin, Texas.

Cret began his architectural studies in Lyon, where he was born. Having won the Paris Prize, he was admitted to the École des Beaux-Arts in Paris, where he won numerous honors. He came to Philadelphia in 1903 to teach at the University of Pennsylvania. In 1914, he returned to France and fought as a private with the Chasseurs Alpins. In 1919, having resumed his post at the University, he and his wife established their home in West Philadelphia. He took an active interest in the Alliance Française and the French Benevolent Society, of which he was director and president from 1923 to 1940. He was made Officier de la Légion d'Honneur and received the Croix de Guerre; he was a member of the American Philosophical Society, the National Academy, the Society of Beaux-Arts Architects and other organizations.

In 1938, the American Institute of Architects gave Cret its highest award, the Gold Medal, of which he was then the only living holder in the United States. The accompanying citation bore these words: "Once again, as in the days of Washington, our architectural heritage is enriched by the presence among us of a distinguished Frenchman."

From the northwest corner of City Hall, at 15th Street and John F. Kennedy Boulevard, one can view the entire length of the Parkway, with the Greek Revival temple of the Philadelphia Museum of Art roughly a mile distant. Except in winter, the view is through the nearby plume of water arching skyward from the adjacent J. F. Kennedy Plaza. That square is better known to Philadelphians as Love Park for Robert Indiana's iconic sculpture, which has found its home in this City of Brotherly Love since 1978.

Facing Logan Square at 18th Street and the Parkway is the Cathedral Basilica of Saints Peter and Paul, a magnificent and imposing brownstone edifice in the Roman Corinthian style. Begun in 1846 and completed in 1884, its admirable interior was designed by Napoléon Le Brun—the same gifted architect who gave Philadelphia the Church of St. Augustine, the Academy of Music, and the handsome Bertrand Gardel monuments at Mount Vernon Cemetery. Over the altar is an ornate baldachino in the Italian Renaissance style.

Here on Logan Circle—Philadelphia's Place de la Concorde [see The French in Philadelphia : Highlights]—are, in addition to the Free Library, two additional cultural institutions of national importance. On the south side, at 19ᵗʰ Street, is the Academy of Natural Sciences. Founded in 1812, its location at this site dates from 1876. The ANS is a museum as well as an educational and research institution. The core of its collection contains over fifteen million specimens charting environmental and evolutionary changes over millions of years. Its library holds some 200,000 scientific volumes and more than 250,000 archival items, including personal and unpublished materials. Hours are 10 a.m. to 4:30 p.m. Monday through Friday, 10 a.m. to 5 p.m. on weekends. For more information, see www.acnatsci.org.

Cathedral Basilica of Saints Peter and Paul

On the west side of Logan Square, at 222 North 20ᵗʰ Street, is the Franklin Institute. Founded in 1824 to promote the mechanical arts and industry, its new home at this location opened in 1933. Since then, it has served as a science museum with special appeal to children and young adults, since its main purpose is to stimulate science education. It contains the Fels Planetarium for star-gazing and the Tuttleman IMAX Theater for all-encompassing film adventure. Its massive rotunda, built in the manner of Rome's Pantheon, is dominated by a twenty-foot marble statue of Philadelphia's most famous citizen, for this is also the Benjamin Franklin National Memorial and houses many of Franklin's possessions. Hours are 9:30 a.m. to 5:30 p.m. every day, and until 9 p.m on Friday and Saturday for the IMAX Theater only. For more, go to www.fi.edu.

The north side of the Parkway, between 20th and 21st Streets, is the site of what will soon become the new home of the Barnes Foundation. This remarkable treasure-trove of modern, and especially French, art was created in 1922 by Albert Barnes (1872-1951). Having made a fortune in business, this self-made man turned to art collection in 1912. In 1924, the Barnes Foundation galleries, designed by Paul Cret, were opened in Merion, Pennsylvania, just beyond Philadelphia's western limit. Jacques Lipchitz designed seven bas-reliefs for the exterior gallery. The American philosopher John Dewey (a life-long friend of Barnes's) served as the first director of education, since it was always Barnes's intent to make his foundation primarily an educational institution. When the Merion galleries were completed, Barnes transferred to them 710 paintings and an endowment of six million dollars.

In 2005, as a result of a petition brought by the Barnes trustees, a court ordered that the Foundation could be moved to the Parkway. It is expected that the new quarters, once completed, will replicate the organization—perhaps even the plan of the Cret building—mandated by Barnes. Today the collection, with more than 2,000 pieces, is valued at more than six billion dollars. It contains 181 paintings by Renoir, 69 by Cézanne, 60 by Matisse, dozens of works by Degas, Manet, Monet, Picasso, Modigliani, and many others. Its collection of nineteenth- and early twentieth-century French masters is virtually unparalleled outside Paris itself.

Albert Barnes, by the way, was made, first, a Chevalier, then, in 1936, an Officier de l'Ordre National de la Légion d'Honneur by the French government.

A bit farther up the Parkway, at 22nd Street, is the **Rodin Museum (cover photo)**. This lovely building, too, was designed by Paul Cret in cooperation with Jacques Gréber. From its opening in 1929, it has housed the largest collection of works by Auguste Rodin outside Paris. The art and artifacts—which include bronze castings, plaster studies, drawings, prints, letters, and books— were collected and willed to the city by a Philadelphia theater owner and philanthropist, Jules Mastbaum.

The figure of *The Thinker* stands at the entrance to the formal garden, along with the first bronze cast of Rodin's *The Gates of Hell*. Behind the garden is the museum, whose collection includes such well-known pieces as "Les Six Bour-geois de Calais," "Le Baiser," the bust of Balzac, and many original casts and drawings. This delightful little museum is beautifully planned and designed to harmonize with the French ambience of the Benjamin Franklin Parkway. Hours are Tuesday through Sunday, 10 a.m. to 5 p.m. See their website, www.rodinmuseum.org.

Directly across the Parkway from the Rodin Museum is the site for a possible new Calder Museum, which is designed to showcase the work of Alexander Calder (1898-1976). Because this Philadelphia-born creator of mobile and stabile sculpture was the son and grandson of renowned Philadelphia sculptors, all three generations of Calders would be honored here. Alexander Milne Calder (1846-1923) created the giant statue of William Penn that dominates the Philadelphia skyline atop City Hall; he and his assistants also produced the hundreds of sculptures that adorn that building. His son, Alexander Stirling Calder (1870-1945), brought the beautiful **Swann Memorial Fountain** at Logan Circle into being. *Ghosts,* one of the large mobiles created by his son, Alexander ("Sandy") Calder, hangs in the Great Stair Hall of the Philadelphia Museum of Art.

It is the work of this third Calder, who spent much of his adult life in France, that will dominate the new museum if the plan for it comes to fruition. Some 300 sculptures, 55 outdoor works, and more than 3,000 works on paper could be housed in the new facility. Also included would be art from Calder's own collection, which represents a number of twentieth-century modernists, many of whom were his friends.

A Calder mobile

Where the Parkway fades into Kelly Drive at the foot of the Art Museum, Emmanuel Fremiet's gilded Joan of Arc raises her standard in triumph. This celebrated equestrian statue is one of three castings—the others are in the Place des Pyramides in Paris and in Nancy, France—and Philadelphians like to imagine that theirs came first! Fremiet (1824–1910) was a nephew of the celebrated sculptor, François Rude, with whom he worked after study at the Musée d'Histoire Naturelle in Paris. Animals and humans are generally combined in his work. His greatest success came with a series of equestrian statues, including this Jeanne d'Arc.

From 1890 to 1941, the statue stood in a little grove at the east end of the Girard Avenue Bridge; there on each Bastille Day, the French colony held a commemorative ceremony. During World War I the ceremony was tinged with patriotic pride and fervor as well as sadness. But in 1940, France had fallen, and there were only sadness and tears as the Consul of France placed the traditional wreath at the foot of the statue. A sonnet was read, written for the occasion by Pierre Giroud, then the dean of the French colony in Philadelphia:

SONNET À JEANNE D'ARC

O Jeanne, toi, l'honneur de notre vieille France
Prends en pitié ses fils opprimés, abattus;
Rallume dans leurs cœurs le feu de l'espérance,
Fais rejaillir en eux les antiques vertus.
Si forte hier encore, et combien accueillante,
Ta patrie abritait un peuple généreux:
La botte du vainqueur l'écrase, pantelante!

Jeanne, relève-la, rends-lui ses jours glorieux.
Trop souvent elle a vu couler en abondance
Le sang de ses soldats, braves champions du droit,
Ce sang, nous te l'offrons : qu'il féconde la France!
Comme un gage sacré de notre ardente foi,
Bénis-le, garde-le dans ta sainte demeure,
Car nous ne voulons pas que notre France meure.

Shortly after, Girard Avenue was widened, the little grove disappeared, and the statue was moved to its present site.

The **Philadelphia Museum of Art** (below) dominates the Parkway from its hilltop plaza on Fairmount. This enormous

Greek Revival temple was completed in 1928, although the Museum dates from 1876, when it was created for the Centennial of the United States which was held in Philadelphia's Fairmount Park that year. The current building rises where the city's municipal reservoir once stood. Made of golden Minnesota dolomite with a roof of glazed blue tiles, it covers ten acres of land and includes more than 200 galleries. Of particular interest on the exterior is the polychromed terra-cotta frieze in the tympanum of the pediment on the North Wing. The frieze depicts Greek gods in the manner of such decorations on ancient Attic buildings. Leading up from the Parkway to the front plaza, from which there is a magnificent view of the Philadelphia skyline, is a long flight of steps made famous to movie-goers as those where Rocky trained. At the foot of those steps on Eakins Oval is an enormous equestrian statue of George Washington, which dominates the surrounding allegorical figures, native flora and fauna, and fountains. This monument was presented to the city in 1897 by the Society of the Cincinnati of Pennsylvania; the Society's members are descendants of men who were officers in America's Revolutionary War.

The Museum contains more than 300,000 works of art from every continent and historical epoch. It is rich in nearly every period of French art. For example, in 1929, the PMA acquired an important collection of Gothic and Renaissance sculpture and art from the French connoisseur, Edmond Foulc. Included were impressive Gothic and Renaissance sculpture and furniture and an alabaster choir screen, dated 1535–50, from the chapel of the Château de Pagny. In 1986, acquisition of the McIlhenny collection added an unmatched trove of nineteenth-century French paintings to already impressive holdings. Among the many French works are beautiful period rooms and a cloister from the south of France. Museum hours are Tuesday through Sunday, 10 a.m. to 5 p.m., and until 8:45 p.m. on Friday. For more information, go to www.philamuseum.org.

A few blocks northeast of the Art Museum, lying roughly between 20th and 25th Streets with an entrance onto the grounds at Girard Avenue, is the fascinating campus of Girard College. This boarding school for students of limited means is the chief legacy visible today of that remarkable French *émigré*, Stephen Girard [see The French in Philadelphia: Highlights]. He left the bulk of his vast fortune for the purpose of founding such a school. Originally, it was for the benefit of poor fatherless boys aged ten to eighteen; today, the school is open to students of both sexes and all races. The college continues to hold a unique place in American education.

Founder's Hall, Girard College (above) is a magnificent Greek Revival temple built in 1833–1847. Once it was completed, Girard's remains were brought here from the graveyard of Holy Trinity Church, where he had been interred after his death in December 1831. They were placed in a sarcophagus in the vast entry hall of the new building; the tomb is surmounted by a statue of Girard by François-Victor Gavelot and flanked by the French and American flags. Upstairs is a collection of Girard's personal effects: his furniture, silverware, dishes, paintings of his ships and portraits of the Chinese merchants with whom he traded. The books from his library show his interest in the French *philosophes* he so admired. The gig in which he drove about town is also on display. Founder's Hall may be visited by appointment. For further information, phone 215-787-2600 or go to http://girardcollege.schoolwires.com.

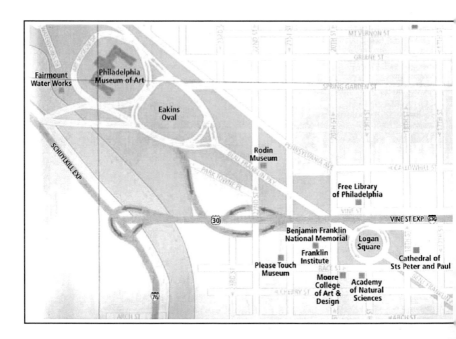

Benjamin Franklin Parkway & the Art Museum Area
(National Park Service, U.S. Department of the Interior)

RITTENHOUSE SQUARE & DELANCEY PLACE

When William Penn's public squares were renamed in 1825, what had been Southwest Square was changed to honor David Rittenhouse (1732-96), a native of nearby Germantown, who became America's first astronomer, first director of the United States Mint, and an early president of the American Philosophical Society. Nearly a century later, Rittenhouse Square—like Washington, Logan, and Center Squares—was enhanced by the attentions of noted Frenchmen. Since then, it has been one of the most beautiful and urbane public squares in America.

In the beginning, this plot of land was just a wooded area; then, while the bustling city still lay mostly to the east, it became a grazing ground. In 1840, it just missed becoming the site of an astronomical observatory. The Victorian Era added a huge iron fountain and an iron watering trough. Meanwhile, the surrounding streets were being filled with more and more stately residences of the rich. Although the mansions took advantage of the bucolic views here, Rittenhouse Square itself was in need of a facelift by the end of that century. With plans for a Paris-inspired grand boulevard in the air [see Benjamin Franklin Parkway & the Art Museum Area], local leaders concluded that the Parc Monceau in Paris would serve as the best model for a makeover.

One of those civic-minded project organizers went to Paris in 1912, and with the help of Jacques Gréber, the architect of the Parkway, she took the necessary pictures of the Parc Monceau. The work proceeded in earnest from 1913 to 1918. Paul Cret, once returned from World War I, was engaged as the architect. Trees were planted, flower beds were laid out, walks and entrances were planned. As intended, the final result did resemble its Parisian counterpart. The magnificent Barye statue, *The Lion Crushing a Serpent* (below) was reset and became a centerpiece of the park. That bronze sculpture had been recast around 1890 from the 1832 original, which is on display in the Salle de Barye in the Louvre.

Antoine-Louis Barye (1796-1875) had at first received much criticism for his use of animals to symbolize human

feelings—a radical departure in art at the time. Eventually, his brilliance as an *animalier* was recognized; he was made a chevalier de la Légion d'Honneur in 1823. He had an enthusiastic following in the United States, including some who formed the American Barye Monument Association to rectify what they thought was his insufficient recognition in his native France. That Association succeeded in erecting a monument to Barye in 1884, designed by the architect Bernier, on the Île Saint-Louis in Paris. Théophile Gautier said of Barye: "He exaggerates, he simplifies, he idealizes the animals and their style; he has a fiery manner, energetic and bold, in fact [he is] like a Michelangelo of the menagerie."

Rittenhouse Square itself has remained virtually unchanged in the near century since this last remodeling. The central pool remains the one designed by Paul Cret. Since 1919, children have loved climbing onto the back of Billy, the goat (other sculpture in the Rittenhouse menagerie includes the Duck Girl and a Giant Frog). The mansions of the Van Rensselaers, Drexels, Earles, Cassatts, and others that once surrounded the square have either been replaced by high-rise buildings or now house businesses and institutions. (The house where the American artist Mary Cassatt [1844-1926] resided when she came from her home in France to see her family stood on the site of today's Rittenhouse Hotel.) Several of those that remain can be visited. They include the former Wetherill mansion, just below the square at 251 South 18th Street, now the home of the **Philadelphia Art Alliance**; the

houses that wrap around the corner of 18th and Locust Streets, occupied since 1924 by the **Curtis Institute of Music** (the main building was a Drexel residence); and the Anthropologie store on the northwest corner of 18th and Walnut Streets, the former Van Rensselaer mansion. A visit to the square on any day when the weather is fair still reveals it as the counterpart to Paris's Luxembourg Garden—teeming with the life of nearby residents, old and young, rich and poor.

The blocks leading into Rittenhouse Square make up Rittenhouse Row, where some of the city's smartest shops, as well as its most popular bars, cafés, and restaurants are located. Thanks to its assortment of sidewalk cafés and French-flavored dining options, the area has been officially recognized since 1999 as Philadelphia's French Quarter (see the orange markers beneath green street signs at several intersections north of the square). French hostelries are repre-sented with Sofitel Philadelphia, at 120 South 17th Street, where

the inviting brasserie is Chez Colette. The Rittenhouse Hotel, facing the park on the west side, is home to the acclaimed Lacroix restaurant. On Walnut Street are George Perrier's Le Bec-Fin, at 1523, and his Brasserie Perrier, at 1619. Nearby are **Rouge (205 South 18th Street)**, Bleu (227 South 18th), Le Jardin (251 South 18th), Le Castagne (1920 Chestnut), La Crêperie (1722 Sansom), La Cigale Café Français (113 South 18th), La

Colombe Torrefaction (130 South 19th), and Le Bus Bakery (135 South 18th).

The streets around Rittenhouse Square—especially those to the south, away from the business district—are still filled with many beautiful mid-nineteenth-century houses. Some remain private homes; others are now apartment houses. Two brown-stone churches from the same period, both designed by John Notman, reflect the neighborhood's elegance, then and now. Holy Trinity faces the northwest corner of Rittenhouse Square; St. Mark's is at 17th and Locust Streets.

The quiet stretch of Delancey from 18th to 21st Streets remains today, as it has been from the 19th century, one of Philadelphia's richest and most elegant residential sections. Many single-family residences remain here. The Nobel-winning novelist, Pearl S. Buck, lived in one of these townhouses; pianist Rudolf Serkin—a long-time director of the Curtis Institute of Music—in another.

At number 2010, a grand, double-width house is now the **Rosenbach Museum and Library**. This was the twentieth-century home of the two Rosenbach brothers. Philip was a leading collector of antiquities, and A. S. W. became one of the world's premier bibliophiles. With their deaths in the 1950s, their long-time home was opened to the public. Today, it remains an exquisitely furnished townhouse that also contains a remarkable library, one that is still expanding. Among its eclectic treasures are the manuscripts of James Joyce's *Ulysses*, Charles Dickens's *Pickwick Papers*, and more than 10,000 drawings and manuscripts of the children's author and illustrator, Maurice Sendak. The living room of poet Marianne Moore's Greenwich Village apartment has been recreated here.

Among the furniture, china, silver, paintings, books, and manuscripts are many French pieces. These include an American French Empire-style wash stand from Joseph Bonaparte's house, a pair of Louis XV child *bergères* (wing chairs), a superb

Louis XVI alabaster clock, a Simon Guillaume commode (circa 1765), and Louis XV French Provincial chairs, along with sculpture by Antoine Bourdelle and Sèvres porcelain. Also here are drawings by Boucher, Fragonard, Gavelot, Daumier, Doré, and a medieval *Book of Hours* (French, Tours School) that is a jewel in itself. Among the letters are one in French by Mary Queen of Scots (who was also the queen consort of François II of France), several by Lafayette, and the cover letter signed by Silas Deane which accompanied a copy of the Declaration of Independence sent to the court of Louis XVI in France. For information, phone 215-732-1600 or go to www.rosenbach.org.

A short distance west on Delancey at 22nd Street there stood, from the early 1890s to some time in the 1920s, a French church, l'Eglise du Saint Sauveur. The church was established by the Reverend Charles Miel (1818–1902), a French Protestant Episcopal pastor. He was a man of deep culture and an excellent speaker; he attracted people of all faiths to his church. In his autobiography, *Le Pèlerinage d'une Âme*, he tells the story of his life and the debt he owed to his early Jesuit training. After his death in 1902, the church lost its *éclat*. In the 1920s the building was torn down; twenty years later, the congregation ceased to exist.

Meanwhile, however, came assurance that the French language and culture would be continued in Philadelphia. In 1903, the Alliance Française de Philadelphie was organized by a group of Francophiles under the leadership of Professor Pierre F. Giroud [see Benjamin Franklin Parkway]. Giroud had come to the United States in about 1900. His ability as a teacher and lecturer was immediately recognized, as was his leadership skill. Among the group of prominent Philadelphians who assisted him in organizing the Alliance was the sister-in-law of Mary Cassatt. For over a century, the Alliance has presented prominent French writers, artists, travelers, actors, and speakers. It provides scholarships for students of French and administers two campuses—in Center City and at Bryn Mawr College—for its classes in the French language. From its inception, the Alliance has found its home in the Rittenhouse Square area. Today, its offices are at 1420 Walnut Street. For more information, phone 215-735-5283, or go to www.alliancefrancaisephiladelphia.com.

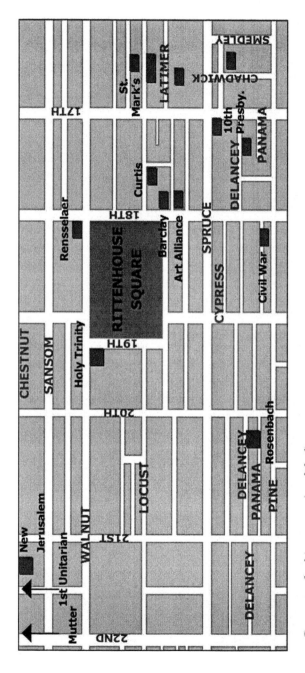

Courtesy of ushistory.org (modified)

WEST PHILADELPHIA

Across the Schuylkill River from Center City lies West Philadelphia. This part of the city grew rapidly in the late 19th century, especially with the decision to move the campus of the University of Pennsylvania here, where space was available, after the Civil War. Today's University City, to the south of 30th Street Station and spreading westward from the river, is home to two important universities: Penn (as the University of Pennsylvania is familiarly known) and Drexel University. Both have grown so much that their borders touch at around 34th and Chestnut Streets.

Amazingly, but—as Philadelphians know—typically, it was Benjamin Franklin who was responsible for founding the University of Pennsylvania. His innovative *Proposals for the Education of Youth in Pensilvania* was designed to go beyond the then-usual focus on educating individuals for the clergy by preparing students for lives of business and public service. The school began as an Academy in 1749, became a college in 1755, and a university—the first in the nation—in 1795. The nation's first medical school was established at Penn in 1765. In 1784, France's Louis XVI donated books to the library, thanks no doubt to Franklin's connection to the French court at the time. Its early buildings, in Center City, were designed by William Strickland (architect of the Second Bank of the United States and the Merchants' Exchange, [see Independence Park]). Today University City includes buildings designed by Frank Furness, Louis Kahn, Eero Saarinen, and the firm of Robert Venturi and Denise Scott Brown. Over the past century, eighteen members of its faculty have received Nobel prizes. The world's first all-electronic computer, ENIAC, was created at Penn.

On the southeast corner of 33rd and Spruce Streets is the University of Pennsylvania's recently expanded Museum of Archaeology and Anthropology, one of the leading institutions of its kind in the nation. With a rich collection of antiquities from Egypt, Babylon, Asia and Meso-America, along with North American Indian artifacts—mostly acquired from the archaeological expeditions it has sponsored—the Museum is well worth a visit. The brilliant and scholarly French abbé Léon Legrain worked for many years at the Museum deciphering ancient tablets. A prominent member of the French colony, he was an officer of the Alliance Française and the French Benevolent Society.

Diagonally across from the Museum, at the northwest corner of 34th and Spruce Streets, is the jagged silhouette of **Irvine Auditorium**; some have thought it is strangely reminiscent of Mont-Saint-Michel! The Auditorium, designed by Horace Trumbauer, is home to one of the largest organs in the world.

At 118 South 36th Street is Penn's Institute of Contemporary Art, which is dedicated to the presentation of the work of emerging and established conporary artists. The Institute's changing exhibitions are open to the public. In addition, the ICA supports commissions, educational programs, and publications relevant to its mission. Hours are Wednesday through Friday, noon to 8 p.m., and Saturdays and Sundays from 11 a.m. to 5 p.m. For more information, go to www.icaphila.org.

An unexpected French connection lies within Penn's School of Dental Medicine at 240 South 40th Street. The new Schattner Center links the Evans Building, which was built on the site of the boyhood home of the School's first major benefactor, to newer research and classroom space. Dr. Thomas William Evans (1823–1897) went to Paris in the 1860s as an assistant to an American dentist established there. Before long, he became dentist to Emperor Napoléon III, the Empress Eugénie, and eventually to many of the crowned heads of Europe. Evans's talent for absolute discretion resulted in his becoming an unofficial diplomat and confidant of royalty. By judicious investments and remarkable business acumen, he built an immense fortune; his magnificent home in Paris was the social center of the American colony.

In 1870, after the defeat at Sedan, Eugénie called on Dr. Evans for help when she was obliged to flee. It was in his coach that she managed to escape before the arrival of the Prussians. The coach is in the possession of Penn's Dentistry School, as is the princely collection of gifts presented to Dr. Evans by his royal patients. Many of these items are on display in the atrium of the Schattner Center. Thomas Evans engaged in many charitable and social enterprises, such as developing the field hospital and tents which provided for better care of the wounded soldiers in the European wars and the American civil war. Although he and his wife lived for decades in Paris, they are buried near the Penn campus in Woodlands Cemetery.

Woodland Terrace is a charming little street near Baltimore Avenue and 41st Street. Most of its twenty original Victorian era houses remain; they are made graceful by the Italianate influence. At number 516 lived Philadelphia's important French architect of the early 20th century, Paul Cret, and his wife [see Benjamin Franklin Parkway and Rittenhouse Square].

Paul Cret House

At the end of the 19th and beginning of the 20th centuries, there stood, on the north side of Walnut between 33rd and 34th Streets, a fine French *pension de famille.* From the time of the French Revolution, there had always been at least one such *pension* in Philadelphia, but this one was probably the last of its kind. The hosts were Monsieur and Madame Allard, who had come to America from Bordeaux with a small fortune but, since they were impractical, it had melted away. So the couple established their pension. The *pension* "Chez Madame Allard" attracted university professors, engineers, lawyers, and business people who wanted to "keep up their French." Monsieur Allard gave French lessons and led the conversation while at table. The boarders were an international group of American, Swedish, German, and French people who remained loyal friends of the Allards and of each other, long after the pension ceased to exist.

Drexel University came into being as the result of the vision of one of nineteenth-century America's most influential financiers, Anthony J. Drexel. Created in 1890 to advance the cause of trade and technical education, the school has maintained its strong emphasis on business, engineering, and science as it has evolved into a university over the course of the past century.

From the beginning, Anthony Drexel regarded knowledge of the arts as essential to education, and as early as 1892, this enormously wealthy Philadelphian—whose mansion was at 39th and Walnut—purchased art for display at the institute (his immigrant father had been a Philadelphia portrait painter). That became the core of a collection that is still on display on the third floor of the ornate Main Hall, at 32nd and Chestnut Streets. In addition to a beautiful tall-case clock made by David Rittenhouse, there are paintings by Charles-François Daubigny and Jules Dupré of the Barbizon School, Napoléon's chess table, and a Sèvres tea and coffee service that belonged to King Louis-Philippe. A popular favorite is **Frédéric-Auguste Bartholdi's bronze statue** *The Water Boy,* whose right toe is brightly polished by students who rub it at exam time for good luck. Bartholdi is better known as the French creator of the Statue of Liberty. Hours are 3:30 to 5:30 p.m., Monday through Friday; visit www.drexel.edu/drexelcollection.

Drexel and Penn, by the way, are only two of more than a dozen institutions of higher learning in Philadelphia. Within the metropolitan region as a whole are more than forty such centers of higher education, which makes the area the nation's leader in the field.

FAIRMOUNT PARK

Fairmount Park is one of the largest municipal parks in the world. From the Benjamin Franklin Parkway and the Art Museum, it spreads north along both banks of the Schuylkill River, then up the rugged gorge of the Wissahickon past Roxborough and Germantown, on through Chestnut Hill to the city's northwestern limits at the beautiful Morris Arboretum. It contains the nation's oldest zoo, an assortment of recreational facilities, two open-air amphitheatres (the Mann Music Center is home to the Philadelphia Orchestra for several weeks in summer; Robin Hood Dell is the site for other popular concerts), and what is regarded to be the finest group of authentic early-American houses in the country.

Behind the Philadelphia Museum of Art and across its driveway, a flight of steps leads down toward the park's Azalea Garden and the Water Works. The steps are flanked by statues of men who aided the Americans during the War of Independence; among them is one of Lafayette.

The **Fairmount Water Works** (foreground) have been nestled against the banks of the Schuylkill River since early in the 19th century. These charming Greek Revival temples were built from 1812 to 1822 to house the paddle wheels and turbine engines of the new public water facility when the one at Center Square became obsolete. For roughly a century, the Fairmount Water Works pioneered the latest technology for distributing water to an ever-expanding city. The Water Works also became the seed for creating the adjacent park. Starting with five acres atop Faire Mount for the new reservoir and public gardens, the park gradually grew larger with bequests and purchases of neighboring land until it reached its present-day size of some 8,000 acres. As the grounds around the Water Works were landscaped with serpentine paths and gardens, Philadelphians came to promenade around these classic structures—and enjoy the views.

The site has long since ceased to supply the city's water. After years of neglect, the entire complex has recently been restored and is now an interpretive center for the history of these buildings and their technology. Castings of the original carved sculptures by William Rush, *Schuylkill Chained* and *Schuylkill Freed*, decorate the entrances to the central pavilions (the originals, with other Rush carvings, are in the Museum of Art just above). Once again, the area is a walker's delight. The interpretive center is open from 10 a.m. to 5 p.m. Tuesday through Saturday and from 1 to 5 p.m. on Sunday. See www.fairmountwaterworks.com.

An easy stroll away are the Azalea Gardens; the graceful Fountain of the Sea Horses, a gift to Philadelphia from the Italian government in honor of the nation's Sesquicentennial, in 1926; the monumental statue of Abraham Lincoln, dating from 1871; and Boat House Row, where most of the city's rowing clubs have been headquartered since the late 19th century. This stretch of the Schuylkill is the nation's premier rowing course. For panoramic views of the riverside from Boat House Row to the Art Museum, the west bank of the Schuylkill River is ideal. At night, the boat houses twinkle with thousands of lights outlining their silhouettes.

Before there was a city park here, these banks of the Schuylkill were a favorite locale for the country homes and estates of wealthy eighteenth- and early nineteenth-century Philadelphians. With easy access to the city by boat, they provided cool alternatives to the crowded city in summer. Among those entertained in these mansions were French visitors of the day, including Lafayette, Joseph Bonaparte, the duc d'Orléans (later, King Louis-Philippe), and other French officers and diplomats. As the city acquired the surrounding land, the historic houses were carefully maintained. Today, some ten of them are furnished with authentic antiques and are open to the public. Among them are the following:

Woodford, one of the Fairmount Park houses open to visitors.

Lemon Hill: This was originally the 350-acre estate of Robert Morris, financier of the American Revolution, who built a farm and greenhouses here in July 1770. By 1798, his financial empire began to crumble, he was sentenced to Debtors' Prison, and his property was sold to Henry Pratt, son of a Philadelphia portrait painter. Pratt developed the land into one of the region's finest gardens. It was he who built the current house in 1800 in the latest Neoclassical style, naming it for the lemon trees that flourished in the greenhouse. He opened his garden "freely to the public," which soon became one of the "grand resorts of fashionable company in the summer."

Mount Pleasant: In 1761, a Scottish sea captain, John Macpherson, built this country seat in what has ever since been recognized as a masterwork of the Chippendale style. John Adams described the house, after dining there in 1775, as "the most elegant seat in Pennsylvania." The mansion's symmetry and the prominent brickwork of its corner quoins are repeated in the two dependencies, or pavilions, that flank it. Inside, the woodwork is elaborately carved throughout, demonstrating Philadelphia architectural carving at its finest. Benedict Arnold bought Mt. Pleasant as a wedding gift for his bride but was convicted of treason before they could occupy it. The house is furnished with Philadelphia Rococo-inspired furniture from the collection of the Museum of Art.

Strawberry Mansion: This largest of the Fairmount Park houses acquired its name in the mid-nineteenth century when it was a dairy farm serving strawberries and cream to visitors on summer outings from the city. The central portion of the house was built in 1790 in the Federal style; some thirty years later, flamboyant Greek Revival wings were added by another owner, Judge Joseph Hemphill, who entertained John C. Calhoun of South Carolina, Daniel Webster of Massachusetts, and the marquis de Lafayette here. Today the house is furnished with a mixture of Federal, Regency and Empire styles; the attic is filled with antique toys.

Sweetbriar: Built in 1797 by the Philadelphia merchant, Samuel Breck, to escape the yellow fever epidemic that took a terrible toll on the city, Breck made this his year-round residence for the next forty years. The house itself is in the Adam style with floor-to-ceiling windows in the two parlors overlooking the Schuylkill; one of those parlors is furnished in the Etruscan style, based on classical forms, and decorated in the terra cotta and black color scheme of ancient Etruscan wall paintings.

Breck's French connections ran deep. His father was the agent for the French Navy in Boston, and the boy was sent to France under the tutorship of a French officer. He returned to America with a perfect knowledge of the French language and a fine appreciation of its culture. He settled in Philadelphia in 1792, married, and a few years later built his mansion. He became a patron of artist-naturalist Jean-Jacques Audubon and supported many philanthropic community projects. Among the influential French visitors to his home were the vicomte de Noailles, Louis-Philippe and his brothers, Talleyrand and Lafayette. Breck was a Philadelphia legislator, active in cultural associations as a member of the American Philosophical Society, and president of the Athenæum.

For more on the park houses—including their variable hours—see www.philamuseum.org/collections/parkhouse.

Among many other sites worth visiting in Fairmount Park, **Memorial Hall** (rooftop pictured) is one of the most imposing.

It is the only remaining major building left standing from the 1876 Centennial Exposition, which marked the first century of America's independence. During the Centennial, this French-inspired Beaux-Arts style building displayed the art collection that then became the basis of the Philadelphia Museum of Art. Memorial Hall is now being renovated to serve as the home of the Please Touch Museum. The surrounding grounds still provide some reminders of the 1876 Exposition, which attracted more than ten million visitors to displays housed in 249 buildings. The statuary honoring Civil War heroes at the exhibition grounds' main entrance is a sampling of the more than two hundred pieces of sculpture that are scattered about Fairmount Park.

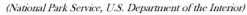

(National Park Service, U.S. Department of the Interior)

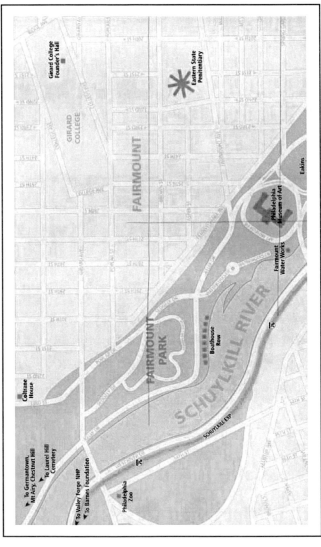

GERMANTOWN & CHESTNUT HILL

In the northwestern reaches of Philadelphia, bordering Wissahickon Creek, are two distinctive neighborhoods with rich histories. Germantown was originally an independent town, settled as early as 1683 by Dutch and German immigrants. Chestnut Hill, lying beyond Germantown toward the city limits, was not developed until the 19th century, and came into being largely as a suburb for the well-to-do. Today, its business district along Germantown Avenue still maintains its charming, late nineteenth-century character. One can shop here for distinctive goods at an unhurried pace.

In Germantown, a number of historic houses on or near Germantown Avenue are open to the public. Among them, several are connected to important individuals or events in America's history. **Stenton**, at 4601 North 18th Street, was the early eighteenth-century plantation home of James Logan (1674–1751), who was William Penn's indispensable assistant. At an early age, Logan accompanied Penn to America as his secretary. Over the next fifty years, he held any number of important positions in the proprietary government, from mayor of Philadelphia to acting governor of the province. He had a brilliant mind, engaged in botanical research that gained him recognition from Linnæus (the "Father of Taxonomy"), and acquired one of the largest libraries in America. Since Logan's death, his books and manuscripts have been preserved by the Library Company of Philadelphia. Stenton, which was completed in 1730, remained in the Logan family until early in the 20th century. Furnished today with many Logan pieces, this unusually authentic house is open to visitors from April 1 to December 15. For hours, phone 215-329-7312, or go to www.stenton.org.

A plainer eighteenth-century house is **Grumblethorpe**, at 5267 Germantown Avenue. It was built in 1744 as the summer home of one of the sons (John) of German immigrants named Wüster. John anglicized the family name as Wister, whereas his brother Caspar spelled the name as Wistar, thereby distinguishing two branches of what has been a distinguished American family ever since. John Wister (1708–1781) was a wine merchant who maintained an orchard and vegetable garden on the property. Successive generations of Wisters for the next two hundred years added flower gardens and a kitchen ell and workshop to the rear of the house. Telephone 215-843-4820 for opening days and times, or go to www.philalandmarks.org.

In an odd coincidence, the **Deshler-Morris House** at 5442 Germantown Avenue saw important service in both the British and the American cause during the late 18ᵗʰ century. Built in 1773, the rather austere house with its "plain Dorick Frontispiece" was occupied during the Battle of Germantown—in October 1777—by the British General Sir William Howe. Sixteen years later, with the new nation's independence won, President George Washington lived and worked here for the summer to escape the plague of yellow fever then ravaging the capital city a few miles below. The next summer, the Washingtons returned, moving two wagonloads of their furniture up to Germantown for their stay. Today, the house is fully furnished with period pieces, some of which may have been in the house when it served as "the first summer White House." For hours of opening, phone 215-596-1748 or go to www.nps.gov/inde.

Wyck, at 6026 Germantown Avenue, was built in about 1690 and remained the home of the Quaker Haines-Wistar family for almost three centuries thereafter. Nearly every generation added to or altered this unusual and distinctive house in some way, building and rebuilding toward the back of the lot. In the 1820s, one of the  leading architects of the time, William Strickland, rearranged the interior to make a more commodious dwelling. The adjoining ornamental garden was laid out in the same period; the original planting scheme has been maintained to the present, making it one of the oldest documented gardens still being cultivated in the nation today. Visitors can obtain an unmatched sense of the domestic lives of a single family over nine generations. For information, phone 215-848-1690, or go to www.wyck.org.

The **Johnson House**, at 6306 Germantown Avenue, is notable architecturally as a rare survival of old Germantown building traditions. Completed in 1768, it sits directly on the street and is characterized by its heavy pent eave above the first floor that runs across the front and side of the house and its simple "Dutch" door topped with a pedimented hood. The property is also notable for its importance nearly a century after it was built as a stop on the Underground Railroad, that system maintained by abolitionists in the years leading up to the Civil War to assist runaway slaves in their escape to freedom. The Johnsons were Quakers and prominent among others who made Philadelphia a stronghold of the anti-slavery movement. During the 1850s, James Johnson sheltered runaway slaves here until they could proceed to freedom farther north. For opening times, call 215-843-0943 or see www.philadelphiahistoricnw.org.

At 6401 Germantown Avenue, **Cliveden** is an elegant 1767 house built in the Palladian style. It was designed as the summer residence of Benjamin Chew (1722–1810), who would soon become chief justice of the province's Supreme Court. Ten years after the house was built, it became the centerpiece of the Battle of Germantown when several companies of British soldiers, falling back from the advance of General George

Washington and his army through Germantown, seized the house on October 4, 1777. The British quickly made it a fortified position from which they could not be dislodged. Washington's attack failed, and the Americans were forced to retreat to Valley Forge and the darkest winter of their effort to achieve independence. Once Cliveden was recovered and restored—and rebought by Benjamin Chew, who had sold it following the battle—it remained the residence of the Chew family until the 1970s, through seven generations.

The impressive entrance hall of the mansion features a screen of Doric columns that deliberately evokes those in the courtroom of what today is known as Independence Hall. Much of the elaborate furniture of the Chew family remains on display throughout the house. Both inside and out, cannonball scars from the Battle of Germantown are still visible. Telephone 215-848-1777 for Cliveden's opening days and times, or go to www.cliveden.org.

The marquis de Lafayette was a guest at Cliveden at the time of his triumphal return to the United States in 1824–25. On that occasion, he was en route to revisit the site of his famous 1778 escape, with 2,200 men, from a British trap at Barren Hill, just beyond modern Chestnut Hill. A gala cortege was organized to accompany him out Germantown Pike, with General A. L. Roumfort, whose French father had come to America in 1800, commanding the Lafayette Guards. Ten years later, on September 9, 1834, another grand parade was organized to commemorate "Lafayette Day" (now an annual event). This time, General Roumfort commanded a battalion formed by the troop of cavalry from Barren Hill, the Lafayette Guards of Chestnut Hill, and "Blues" from Germantown.

More than a century later, in May 1976, the Historical Societies of Conshohocken and Plymouth Meeting organized yet another celebration to commemorate Lafayette's successful maneuver. In this year of the Bicentennial of the United States there were in the cortege American soldiers, the French War Veterans Association, the Honorary French Consul in Philadelphia, a representative of the New York Consulate, officers and members of the Alliance Française de Philadelphie, and many civic organizations. This long and colorful procession again retraced the famous route, placing permanent markers as they went. Once more Cliveden was the scene of a fine reception to commemorate Lafayette's earlier visit. The guest of honor was comte de Lafayette, a descendant of the Revolutionary hero. The Philadelphia city Troop led the guests to Wyck, where honor was again paid to the marquis de Lafayette. A comparable commemorative celebration is scheduled for 2006. Meanwhile, in 2002, the United States Congress bestowed honorary citizenship on Lafayette, making him only the sixth such person in the nation's history to receive that honor.

Another Frenchman, Count Jean du Barry, had a less lasting impact on the United States. In 1803, he purchased land in what was then a very rural Chestnut Hill and built an estate there. After he had embellished the grounds with flowers—mainly roses, boxwood, shrubs and trees from France—it became known as the most picturesque garden in the vicinity. Because du Barry had noticed that wild mulberry trees grew there in profusion, he concluded that he might foster a silk industry in America by raising silk worms. After importing worms from France, he discovered that they refused to eat these mulberry leaves, so promptly died, along with du Barry's dream of local silk production.

For whatever reason, Chestnut Hill has sometimes attracted a French look in its architecture, as is evident on a drive through many of its residential streets. An early example can be found at

the corner of Emlen Street and Allens Lane. The houses are in the **Norman style** and create a little French enclave surrounded by a beautiful stone wall. Set into the wall, to complete the picture, is a stone with the legend « Défense d'Afficher » ["Post No Bills"].

At the northwesternmost corner of Chestnut Hill, the Morris Arboretum of the University of Pennsylvania is a 92-acre preserve for thousands of rare plants. In this Victorian landscape are many of Philadelphia's oldest, rarest, and largest trees. For hours, go to www.morrisarboretum.org.

COUNTRY MANSIONS & GARDENS

Philadelphia's suburbs are rich in history and natural beauty. To the north of the city, Bucks County sprawls along the rugged Delaware River where still-bucolic stretches reveal the peaceful landscapes that have long nurtured artists (the New Hope school of impressionists worked here in the early 20th century) and writers (Oscar Hammerstein, Moss Hart, James Michener, and S. J. Perelman all lived here). Pennsbury Manor, the fascinating recreation of William Penn's plantation home, is open to visitors. The proprietor himself journeyed from here down the Delaware to Philadelphia in a remarkable barge, now on exhibit in one of the estate's outbuildings. For hours, phone 215-946-0400 or go to www.pennsburymanor.org.

In many suburban places, French connections and influences are evident. Just beyond Philadelphia's city limits in Montgomery County is the **Barnes Foundation**, in Merion. Although this remarkable collection of French Impressionist and other paintings is scheduled to move to the Parkway [see Benjamin Franklin Parkway], it remains for now in its original home designed by Paul Cret. For hours and reservations, phone 610-667-0290, or go to www.barnesfoundation.org.

Several miles farther west is Mill Grove, the first home in America of Jean-Jacques (John James) Audubon (1785-1851). The property was owned by Audubon's father, who sent his son here to manage the estate. It was here that the young man became fascinated by America's wildlife, particularly the birds. In France, he had studied painting briefly with Jacques-Louis David; in Pennsylvania, encouraged by Thomas Sully and Gilbert Stuart, Audubon found his true vocation in painting the birds of America. Many of his famous prints and mementos of his life are displayed at Mill Grove, which is now the center of the Audubon Wildlife Sanctuary. For mansion visiting hours, phone 610-666-5593, or go to www.montcopa.org/historicsites.

Almost next door to Mill Grove is Valley Forge National Historical Park, which was the encampment for the Continental Army during a dark six months beginning in December 1777 and following the American retreat from the Battle of Germantown. Here, Washington's army, poorly equipped and ill-clothed, endured a harsh winter to emerge the following spring as a better-trained force, prepared to face the next years of the war until the final victory was achieved at Yorktown. Visitors to Valley Forge can see much of the encampment as it was more than two hundred years ago. For directions and additional information, go to www.ushistory.org/valleyforge.

A short distance south of Valley Forge is the Duportail House in Chesterbrook. Louis le Begne de Presle Duportail (1743–1802) came to North America in 1777 with three other French engineers. Soon he was given command of the Engineers Corps of the Continental Army with the rank of brigadier general; following the victory at Yorktown, he was promoted to major general. As Chastellux wrote, "the beautiful and well contrived fortress works" at West Point "were planned by two French engineers, Duportail and Gouvion." In May 1780, Duportail was taken prisoner at the capitulation of Charleston, South Carolina, and was later exchanged. He was present and took part in the Westerfield and the Dobbs Ferry conferences before Yorktown.

Back in France in the early years of the French Revolution, Duportail was Minister of War in 1790–91. In 1794, he emigrated to the United States, acquired this farm near Valley Forge, and lived here as a refugee. He died on his return voyage to France in 1802. The restored residence of General Louis Duportail is available for private social functions. For information, phone 610-644-4840.

On the border of Delaware and Chester Counties, Chadds Ford is home to several generations of Wyeth family artists. The Brandywine River Museum houses many Wyeth paintings, including those of N. C. Wyeth, his son, Andrew, and grandson Jamie Wyeth, as well as other artist members of the family and their contemporaries. For hours, phone 610-388-2700, or go to www.brandywinemuseum.org. Adjacent to Chadds Ford is the Brandywine Battlefield Park, the site of a battle in September 1777, in which British forces outmaneuvered Washington's army and continued their march from the Chesapeake to Philadelphia, which they occupied later that same month.

Nemours, one aspect of the estate.

The region between Chadds Ford and Wilmington, Delaware, is notable for the long-time presence of the du Pont family. The founder of the du Pont dynasty in America was Eleuthère Irénée (1772–1834), the son of the leading French economist and physiocrat, Pierre S. du Pont. His son entered the royal powder works at age seventeen and was taught the trade by Lavoisier. Eleuthère left for America during the French Revolution, arriving with his family in 1799, when he began formulating plans to improve the quality of American gunpowder. From his 1802 gunpowder works on the Brandywine grew the formidable E. I. du Pont de Nemours & Company that has been a dominant force in the world's chemical industry for two centuries.

Lafayette was among the original subscribers underwriting the company.

Today, on the site of Eleuthère's original mill is the Hagley Museum in Wilmington, Delaware. Surrounded by a 235-acre estate, the museum provides displays on the history of business and industry as well as a research library with archives on those subjects. For further information, phone 302-658-2400 or go to www.hagley.lib.de.us.

Also near Wilmington in the Brandywine Valley is Winterthur, the estate of Henry Francis du Pont, who amassed an unparalleled collection of American furnishings and decorative arts. This incomparable museum is arranged in period rooms in a variety of styles dating from 1600 to 1800, and may be visited through guided tours. For more information, phone 800-448-3883, or go to www.winterthur.org.

Nearby is another du Pont estate, that of Alfred L. du Pont, also open to the public. Nemours, built in 1909-1910, is a grand mansion in modified Louis XVI style, containing more than a hundred rooms and formal gardens that extend in a vista of one-third of a mile from the main house. The gardens are filled with fountains, pools, and statuary. They rank among the finest in the French style to be found in America. Phone 302-651-6912 for information, or go to www.fieldtrip.com/de.

Back across the Pennsylvania border near Kennett Square is Longwood Gardens on the estate of a fourth-generation Pierre S. du Pont. Regarded as one of the leading horticultural display gardens in the world today, it allows visitors to roam more than a thousand acres of landscaped gardens, woodlands, and meadows. There are twenty distinct outdoor gardens, and four acres of tropical plants in greenhouses. Longwood is open every day of the year and boasts changing seasonal displays. For hours and further information, phone 610-388-1000, or go to their website, www.longwoodgardens.org.

AFTERWORD

The French influence on Philadelphia and the surrounding region is clear, even if it is somewhat subtler than that of certain other nationalities—notably, the English, Irish, and Germans—who came here in greater numbers than the French. Contributions of the French government and of many French citizens were crucial in the 1770s and beyond to America's successful struggle for independence. Among the key players who came to America were such leading French military figures as Rochambeau and Lafayette. Perhaps even more important than their gallantry and military prowess was the intellectual presence at the nation's birth of Montesquieu, Rousseau, and Voltaire, whose ideas profoundly influenced the American polity and character right down to the present day. The spirit of these leading *philosophes* still permeates the atmosphere of Independence Hall, still breathes life into the nation's Constitution and the entire American political system.

The presence in eighteenth-century Philadelphia of the French officers, the diplomatic corps, and the refugees gave a new, sophisticated focus to Philadelphia's social life at the time, helping to make this the most cosmopolitan American city of the period. Beginning with Chastellux and Moreau de Saint-Méry—who were followed with the journals and reports of such writers as Chateaubriand, Tocqueville, and Crèvecœur—French commentators have held up a mirror to America so that Americans could see themselves as others did, and learn from them as a result.

French influence on this area has been broader still. It has graced the architecture of important buildings, left its imprint on parks and boulevards, and served both to whet and satisfy the appetites of Philadelphians, literally and figuratively. French citizens and immigrants to America continue to make important contributions to the commercial and civic life of the city and the region. Some of the finest art produced in France now has a home in this region for Philadelphians—and visitors from all over the world—to enjoy. The French connection endures.

* * * * * * *

My goal for this unique guide was to make it useful in discovering the many French connections to contemporary Philadelphia and its suburbs. I have sought to complement the examination of the historic contributions of the French that Annette Emgarth provided in her two releases of *French Philadelphia,* in 1976 and 1991. Therefore, I have added information for places that were not included previously—some of which did not then exist—and I have expanded or updated earlier information. This information typically has come from the sites themselves, usually by way of their websites, whose addreses are now included in the text, as appropriate. The Emgarth narrative has been somewhat rearranged for a more coherent presentation of this larger work which contains half again as much material.

I have made several corrections to the Emgarth text. One or two dates were in error and have been corrected. Two other changes are more substantive. The first, in the Independence Park section, corrects the date of the lavish Fête du Dauphin hosted by the French Minister, the marquis de la Luzerne. The party occurred in August 1782, not July 1781, as stated in the earlier publications. It seems only logical that this party in honor of the birth, in October 1781, of an heir to the French throne could only have taken place some time after the dauphin was born rather than several months before that event (given the slowness of communication in the 18th century, the news of the royal birth did not even reach Philadelphia until the spring of 1782). Emgarth's error was not her own, but had been made by her source, the earlier essayist Agnès Repplier.

The second correction, in the Society Hill section, now makes clear that it was Emma Bouvier Drexel's step-daughter, the future St. Katharine Drexel, rather than Emma herself, who raised millions of dollars to assist in the education of native Americans and African-Americans.

FRANCO-AMERICAN SOCIETIES IN PHILADELPHIA

The following associations contribute much to present-day interest in the French language and civilization, which have so greatly enriched this region:

Alliance Française de Philadelphie: Organized in 1903, the Alliance offers programs, open to the public, on every aspect of French culture. Major social events include Mardi Gras and Bastille Day celebrations. The school of the Alliance Française offers a variety of courses at all levels, including immersion courses, French for children and French for travelers. Its teachers are highly trained in the teaching of French as a foreign language. The offices of the Alliance Française are located at 1420 Walnut Street. For more information, phone 215-735-5283, or visit www.alliancefrançaisephiladelphia.com.

Alliance Française de Doylestown: Located in the county seat of Bucks County, Pennsylvania, the Alliance Française de Doylestown offers classes in the French language as well as programs and events relevant to French culture. Phone 215-345-0188 or visit www.websiteagency.com/AFD.

Philadelphie Accueil: This association brings together francophone individuals residing in the Philadelphia region. Its purpose is to help francophone families to become integrated into American life and to accompany them throughout their stay here. The Accueil provides practical information and numerous activities for expatriates in the region. Headquarters are at 745 Clyde Circle, Bryn Mawr, PA 19010. Phone 610-519-0145 or visit their website at www.Philadelphieaccueil.com, where all who seek French connections in the Philadelphia area can find information and useful links.

France – Philadelphie: "Building business, cultural and artistic bridges between France and Philadelphia for 25 years." Located at 1650 Market Street, Suite 2500—One Liberty Place, Philadelphia, PA 19103. Phone 215-851-1474.

The French-American Chamber of Commerce: The Chamber promotes sound, strong trade relations between the United States and France. It is supported by some five hundred business leaders and their companies in the region. The Philadelphia Chamber is the second-largest chapter among twenty-three cities. For more information, visit their website at www.faccphila.org.

French Heritage Society: This organization provides financial support for architecturally significant buildings in the United States and France. The Society also sponsors cultural and educational exchange programs between the two countries. To learn more about the Society's Philadelphia chapter, see www.frenchheritagesociety.org.

The French Benevolent Society of Philadelphia: The Society is one of the oldest charitable organizations in the United States, having been founded in 1793. Historically, it has provided advice and financial assistance to people of French nationality or extraction in Philadelphia, who were suffering from poverty or distress.

L'Union des Français de l'Etranger: Founded in 1927, its mission is to create and maintain ties between people in France and French expatriates in this region.

The French War Veterans Association: This association consists of an active group of veterans who participate in relevant patriotic ceremonies.

American Association of Teachers of French, Philadelphia Chapter: Organized in the 1930s, it brings together some three hundred college, secondary, and primary school teachers of French from both the public and private sectors. Meetings permit teachers to keep abreast of trends in language education. In an annual contest, students compete for oral and written excellence. See www.aatfphila.org and www.frenchteachers.org.

The French International School of Philadelphia: Located in the Philadelphia suburb of Bala Cynwyd, the school gives French and American children the benefits of a true bilingual educational experience. For more information, visit the website www.efiponline.com.

FRENCH COMPANIES IN THE PHILADELPHIA REGION

Today, some fifty French companies operate in the greater Philadelphia region. For complete information on these and the hundreds more with French connections, see The French-American Chamber of Commerce, above.

French Philadelphia

SELECTED BIBLIOGRAPHY

Alberts, Robert C. *The Golden Voyage : The Life and Times of William Bingham 1752-1804.* Boston: Houghton Mifflin, 1969.

Alotta, Robert I. *Street Names of Philadelphia.* Philadelphia: Temple University Press, 1975.

Archives, La Société française de bienfaisance de Philadelphie.

Armes, Ethel. *Nancy Shippen, Her Journal Book. The International Romance of a Young Lady of Fashion of Colonial Philadelphia with Letters to Her and about Her.* Philadelphia: J. B. Lippincott, 1935.

The Athenæum Annals, 158th Annual Meeting Reports. Philadelphia, 1975.

Bach, Penny Balkin. *Public Art in Philadelphia.* Philadelphia: Temple University Press, 1992.

Blanchard, Pierre. *Journal of My Forth-fifth Ascension.* Philadelphia, 1793. Philadelphia: The Penn Mutual Life Insurance Company, 1943.

Borkson, Joseph L. *Philadelphia: An American Paris.* Philadelphia: Camino Books, Inc., 2001.

Brooks, George S. *Friend Anthony Benezet.* Philadelphia: University of Pennsylvania Press, 1937.

Bruns, Roger A. "Anthony Benezet and the Natural Rights of the Negro," *Pennsylvania Magazine of History and Biography.* Philadelphia: The Historical Society of Pennsylvania. January, 1972.

Burt, Struthers. *Philadelphia: Holy Experiment.* Garden City, New York: Doubleday, Doran & Company, 1945.

Chastellux, marquis de. *Travels in North America in the Years 1780, 1781 and 1782.* A revised translation by Howard C. Rice, Jr. 2 vols. Published for the Institute of Early American History and Culture at Williamsburg, Virginia. Chapel Hill: University of North Carolina Press, 1963.

Cret, Paul-Philippe. *Current Biography, 1942.* New York: H. W. Wilson, 1942.

Davis, John H. *The Bouviers.* New York: Farrar, Straus & Giroux, 1969.

De Moyer, Robert, Jr. and James P. Martinelli. *Escape Route of Lafayette from the British at Barren Hill, May 20, 1778.* Conshohocken, Pennsylvania: Lee Tire and Rubber Company, 1975.

Du Pont de Nemours, E. I. *Autobiography of an American Enterprise.* Wilmington, Delaware: du Pont, 1952.

Earle, John J., III. "Talleyrand in Philadelphia, 1794-96," *Pennsylvania Magazine of History and Biography,* July 1967. pages 282-298.

Fairmount Park Association. *Sculpture of a City: Philadelphia's Treasures in Bronze and Stone.* New York: Walker Publishing Co., Inc., 1974.

Frey, Carroll. *The First Air Voyage in America.* Philadelphia: The Penn Mutual Life Insurance Company, 1943.

Hamon, Joseph. *Le chevalier de Bonvouloir.* Paris : Jouve & Cie., 1953.

Herrick, Cheesman A. *Stephen Girard, Founder, Girard College.* Set up and printed in the Trade School, Philadelphia, 1923.

Hornick Nancy Slocum. "Toward a Theory of Full Equality," *Pennsylvania Magazine of History and Biography,* October 1975.

Klein, William M., Jr. *Gardens of Philadelphia and the Delaware Valley.* Philadelphia: Temple University Press, 1975.

Lopez, Claude-Anne. *Mon Cher Papa: Franklin and the Ladies of Paris.* New Haven: Yale University Press, 1966.

MacFarlane, John J. *History of Early Chestnut Hill.* Philadelphia: City History Society, 1923.

McClelland, Jim. *Fountains of Philadelphia.* Mechanicsburg, Pennsylvania: Stackpole Books, 2005.

Miller, Fredric M., Morris J. Vogel, and Allen F. Davis. *Still Philadelphia: A Photographic History, 1890-1940.* Philadelphia: Temple University Press, 1983.

Moreau de Saint-Méry, Médéric-Louis-Elie. *Voyage aux Etats Unis d'Amérique 1793-1798.* New Haven: Yale University Press, 1913.

Moreau de Saint-Méry, Médéric-Louis-Elie. *Moreau de St. Méry's American Journey 1793-1798.* Translated and edited by Kenneth Roberts and Anna M. Roberts. Garden City, New York: Doubleday & Company, 1947.

Moss, Roger W. *Historic Houses of Philadelphia.* Philadelphia: University of Pennsylvania Press, 1998.

Repplier, Agnès. *Philadelphia: The Place and the People.* New York: The Macmillan Company, 1899.

Robin, abbé. *Nouveau voyage dans l'Amérique septentrionale, en l'année 1781 ; et campagne de l'armée de M. le comte de Rochambeau.* Philadelphie : et se trouve à Paris, Chez Moutard, 1782 .

Schiff, Stacy. *A Great Improvisation: Franklin, France and the Birth of America.* New York: Henry Holt and Company, 2005.

Vogel, Maurice J. *Cultural Connections: Museums and Libraries of Philadelphia and the Delaware Valley.* Philadelphia: Temple University Press, 1991.

Watson, John F. *Annals of Philadelphia and Pennsylvania.* Enlarged with many revisions and additions by Willis P. Hazard. 3 vols. Philadelphia: Leary, Stuart, 1924.

Wolf, Edwin, 2nd. *Philadelphia: Portrait of an American City.* Harrisburg, Pennsylvania: Stackpole Books, 1975.

AUTHORS

Annette H. Emgarth (1900–1992) was reared in a bilingual environment which prompted her life-long dedication to the teaching of French. She received bachelor's and master's degrees in Romance Languages from the University of Pennsylvania and taught for thirty-five years in the Philadelphia public schools. She also devised tests for the Modern Language Association for teachers of French, and developed the Pennsylvania State Course of Study in Modern Foreign Languages. She was honored by the French Government with the Palmes académiques and Officier d'Instruction publique awards. She served as the vice president and secretary of the Alliance Française de Philadelphie and as president of the Philadelphia Area Modern Language Association.

Lynn H. Miller, PhD, is Professor Emeritus of Political Science at Temple University, where he was a member of the faculty for thirty-two years, during which time he served terms as president of the Faculty Senate, associate dean of the Graduate School, and chair of the Political Science Department. He has taught at UCLA and the University of Pennsylvania. He began graduate study at the Institut de Hautes Études internationales in Geneva, Switzerland, then received a doctorate from Princeton. Dr. Miller is author or co-author of several books on international politics, as well as numerous articles and reviews; he has also published poetry and fiction. He is a member of the Board of Directors of the Alliance Française de Philadelphie.

French Philadelphia

INDEX

LLC

Web : http://www.beachlloyd.com
Email: BEACHLLOYD@erols.com
Telephone (610) 407-0130 or
1-866-218-3253, PIN 8668
(toll free in the United States)
Fax (775) 254-0633

P.O. Box 2183
Southeastern, PA 19399-2183
USA